"In *The God Connection*, Bethany Hicks gives the reader permission to go on their own unique adventure in hearing the voice of God. In doing so she debunks the false narrative that only the 'chosen ones' can hear and converse with God.

This book not only gives permission to explore, but provides a Biblical roadmap to aid in the journey into a wealth of intimate conversations with the most generous and loving Being in the universe. Read this book with expectation and activate your personal God Connection."

**David Crone**
Senior Leader of The Mission
Author of *Decisions that Define Us,*
*The Power of Your Life Message,*
and *Prisoner of Hope*

# THE GOD CONNECTION
Bethany Hicks

First Edition

Foreword by Dan McCollam

ISBN: 979-8-5289-5263-5

Imprint: Independently published

Cover design by Ryan Biore

Interior design & typesetting by Mario Lampic

# THE GOD CONNECTION

## BETHANY HICKS

*To every*
*son and daughter of God*
*who longs to know*
*His voice better*

# CONTENTS

# FOREWORD

The first great challenge to the human species spawned in the garden of Eden from the question, "Did God really say?" That subtle and deceiving query plagued and diverted the course of humanity for multiple millennia as humankind doubted their ability to hear God's voice. Bethany's book, *The God Connection*, heals the wound of uncertainty and restores the dignity of sons and daughters of God to believe in their God-given ability to recognize and respond to the voice of God. She not only clearly makes the point that every person has an innate God connection, but she unpacks the many ways God speaks making His voice distinct and fully accessible to the reader.

I am writing this forward as a first-hand witness to much of the journey that unlocked the treasure found in these pages. I first met Bethany at a small community church tucked between the majestic peaks of the Sierra Nevada mountains of Central California. People were driving hundreds of miles to be part of a worship and discipleship school she had founded, and as the director of an international worship organization, I had been asked to speak at the graduation. Bethany's strength of leadership, her pioneering spirit, and anointed worship leading prompted me to invite her and her sister Heather (who is also a powerful worship leader) to join our training teams ministering around the world.

The strategist and advancer side of Bethany's prophetic calling accelerated the development of a community of people committed to exploring what following the voice of the Lord could mean as a life skill. We worked with those partnering with the voice of God to serve government, business, family and the church. This season was the formative years for developing the concepts chronicled in The God Connection. The curricula and method that Bethany co-labored in creating has now been used to bless and train multiplied thousands on six different continents.

My hope for you as you read this book is that the simple yet profound concepts of this book will strengthen your God connection. My mentor used to say, "Nothing gives you more dignity than to know you can hear the voice of God." May your life be dignified by the biblical pursuit of knowing and following His voice.

**Dan McCollam**

*Author and international trainer, founder of Sounds of the Nations, co-founder of the Prophetic Company and Bethel School of the Prophets*

# INTRODUCTION

Everyone is hardwired to hear God. You have an inherent, built-in—even *natural* ability—to communicate directly with God. You are born with it. It's not something you have to plead or beg God for. It's not even just for the religious elite or spiritual experts of our day. It is our *right as His sons and daughters to know His voice,* and therefore, every person on the planet is capable of it. There are no hoops you have to jump through or complicated assignments you must accomplish to hear His voice. Hearing God is much simpler than that.

As a young child, I would have this constant inner dialogue with Jesus. I would talk to Him in my heart and mind or write down some thoughts in my journal like He was my top-secret best friend. I wasn't afraid to tell Him anything and would share with Him my hopes and frustrations, interactions about the boy I liked, my agitation with one of my siblings, or anything else that came to my adolescent mind. Don't get me wrong. I was by no means this hyper-spiritual kid who walked in miraculous life-altering encounters with God like Samuel the prophet did as a young child. I just had a simple belief that I could talk to God and that He cared enough to listen even though I never really heard Him speak back to me.

Fast-forward twenty years, I remember watching a few friends of mine encourage other people with how God thinks about them, and it provoked a longing in my heart I wasn't aware I had. Watching my friend's faces as they spoke God's good thoughts to a grateful recipient, I was struck by how confident they seemed in their ability to know they were actually hearing God's voice. Equally fascinating to me was how impacted the receivers of those encouraging words were. I would think, *I want to hear God's voice like that! I want to know that I know that I know that He is speaking to me.* But how? Was this a special gift for the selective few? Were prophets the only ones who could really hear God speak, just like the Bible days? Don't the mountains quake and the heavens thunder in a terrifying way before His voice can be known? Or shouldn't a somber Old-Testament-like prophet point his finger at me in an authoritative way and begin a prophetic discourse with "Thus saith the Lord of hosts unto thee..." as he proceeds to speak God's thoughts and future to me?

It was questions like these and more that provoked me to pursue the voice of God for myself, which ultimately set me on a catalytic path of unhindered connection with God. The day I finally discovered what His voice sounded felt like a light switch had been flipped on in my spirit. Suddenly, I could see all of the times He had *already* been speaking to me throughout the span of my life. I just hadn't realized that *that* was *His* voice! It seemed so natural, so easy, that I had discounted its weight as God actually speaking to me. Looking back, I realized it wasn't that God hadn't already been speaking to me. It was that my expectation of what He *should* sound like was an obstacle to my recognizing His voice.

Too many people are wandering through life like I was without realizing their absolute access to the voice of God. They are making decisions that will affect their future, not realizing that the One who ordained for them a good future and a hope is *already speaking* to them about their destiny.[1]

God's desire from the foundations of the earth is to have regular and intimate communion with those He loves—you and me. The foundation for any true connection is communication. In fact, the greater the level of communication, the greater the degree of connection is possible. There are multiple books and resources available today to help people grow in their ability to communicate with one another. Bestselling books like *The Five Love Languages* by Gary Chapman have been life-changing for many who have read them because they unpack the reality that there are multiple ways to receive and give love. You grow in your connection with a loved one when you take the time to communicate to them in a way that *they* can hear, receive, and understand. It's the same with God and us. God did everything possible on His end to make constant connection available to us a reality through His Son, Jesus Christ, and by His Spirit. We were never intended to live life without full access to His voice. And because God is Love, He has built within you the God connection—your ability to recognize God's voice in a way that you can hear, receive. and understand.

For the purposes of this book, I will frequently be using the term *hardwired,* defined as *being a part of the innermost nature of a person or thing*[2] and also, *pertaining to an intrinsic and relatively unmodifiable behavior pattern* just like a cricket has a hardwired pattern of chirps.[3] How does this apply to our subject? It means that your whole being—spirit, soul, and body—is

---

1   Jeremiah 29:11

2   https://www.dictionary.com/browse/hardwired

3   https://www.dictionary.com/browse/hardwired

created (hardwired) to receive divine revelation directly from God Himself on every dimensional level. Why is this concept of being hardwired important? Because you don't need anything additional outside of what He has already built within you to access His voice. You don't need a special Bible college degree or an angelic encounter to awaken your ability to hear Him. Just as a baby is born with everything it needs to survive and thrive in life, so we are born with full capacity to commune with our Creator. More than that, you are *already* receiving from Him.

I have two goals throughout this book. First, my hope throughout these chapters is that you will discover the primary ways that you are *already* hearing God. Some feel God's presence speaks to them while others may see God speaking through creation. There are those who literally see angels with their physical eyes while others just "know" when something feels true in their spirit. Each of these are powerful ways that God communicates. Secondly, my purpose is to help *expand* your ability to recognize God speaking in ways that you maybe haven't identified before. We are not designed to hear God speak in one way only. There are multiple dimensions that He is speaking, and by expanding our "broadband hearing" experience to recognize His voice, we have the potential to commune with Him in every possible manner.

Each chapter will break down some differing ways that you are hardwired to know God though by no means is this list exhaustive. My hope is that it will spark a recognition within you of the many ways that the Lord has already been speaking or increase newly recognized avenues of His voice. Additionally, you will be given some practical tools to expand your ability to receive His voice on every frequency He is speaking. You are born for this. This is what you've been made for. You are hardwired to receive and respond to all of the ways His voice is speaking in your life, and He wants you to become confident as His son and daughter that you do, in fact, know His voice. This is the God connection, the full assurance that you can—*and already are*—hearing Him.

# CHAPTER 1

## OUR RECEPTORS

H EARING GOD IS NOT a cookie-cutter, one-size-fits-all process. Every person is created uniquely and thus receives information from God differently. God delights in variety as evidenced by creation around us where there are hundreds of thousands of species of flowers with varying shapes, colors and fragrances. In a similar way, each person is fearfully, uniquely, and wonderfully made.[4] Though we are all hardwired to know Him, each of us has our own diverse ways we connect with His voice.

> *Each one should use whatever gift he has received to serve others, faithfully administering God's grace in its various forms.*
>
> *I Peter 4:10*

One of my children's favorite pastimes is to get our pet Australian Shepherd all riled up when I'm about to take him on a run. They will start telling him in excited tones, *Do you*

---

4    Psalms 139:14

*want to go for a walk? Huh boy? Are you going to go for a run with Mama?* And of course, he gets incredibly excited every time. Now, it doesn't really matter what words they use to speak to him. They could even be reading the dictionary. But if they did it with the same excited tone and body language, he doesn't care what they're saying; he believes he's about to do something exciting.

Humans understand communication in a similar manner. Did you know that the majority of what is heard in a verbal exchange between people is not through the actual words spoken?[5] Tone of voice and body language make up for more than ninety-percent of what is actually understood by the hearer.

The same variety in communication could be applied to people's learning styles. There are many ways that people learn which is why a cookie-cutter template for students in school is not always beneficial for the students. One person may learn best as an auditory learner while others are more visual—they need to see it to learn it. Still others like my son are very kinesthetic, meaning they must actually put action to their studies in order for them to retain it. My daughter needs to be in a quiet place with no one talking in order to effectively learn while I have friends who have always excelled when they did a project with another person. Everyone has a unique mix of learning styles that suits them best.

Based on the above observations and knowledge about human condition and communication, couldn't we say that God absolutely loves variety? And if that is true, why would we think that God would limit Himself to speaking to us in only one way?

---

5    https://www.mindtools.com/pages/article/Body_Language.htm

> *The hearing ear and the seeing eye, the Lord has made*
> *them both.*
>
> Proverbs 20:12

We are not just hearers only; we are also seers, feelers, perceivers, and much more. Because God is the One who uniquely created us, He knows how to speak to each one of us in a way that we can best understand Him.

Your unique ability to communicate with the Lord can be found in your *receptors.* A simple definition of receptor within the human body is a "sense organ."[6] *It is the ability to receive stimuli, or something that quickens action, feeling, thought, etc.* Every person has receptors—spirit, soul, and body receptors, and everyone is receiving information at any given moment through their receptors. Even now, there are millions of receptors that affect our lives by communicating information to us such as hunger, heat, pain, balance, gravity, time, etc. Our receptors are gathering data regularly and contributing to the information overload we receive every day. We in turn make decisions based on the information our receptors deliver and choose to accept.

Our receptors are how we recognize the voice of God. They are the vehicles through which God communicates to us. This is why, I believe, so many of us have discounted God's voice in our lives. It's not that we don't want to hear Him. It's that the way He speaks to us sometimes is so natural, we don't consider it to be supernatural. I like how Dan McCollam defines the supernatural: *"It's God's super and our natural."* God has created all of mankind in His image and as believers, He has placed His Spirit within us so that we can be supernaturally natural in our life exchange with Him.

---

6    https://www.merriam-webster.com/dictionary/receptor

This is why people who don't yet know the Lord can access spiritual information, because they also are created hardwired to receive on every level of their being. Every person comes to Christ by encountering Him at some level before they know Him. This is proof that we are all hardwired for God-encounters. The main difference is that those who don't know the Lord have yet to learn to *recognize* that it is God's voice as the One speaking to them versus other voices in their lives.

Though this concept of discerning God's voice through these primary ways has been taught for many years within the church, I first heard these four simple descriptions several years ago and it really helped de-mystify recognizing His voice for me. Our four primary receptors for receiving from the Lord are:

- Seeing        • Hearing

- Sensing       • Perceiving

Throughout this book we'll explore each receptor in further detail. However, over the years, as my colleagues and I have trained thousands to hear God's voice we have isolated three additional sub-groups within the main receptors through which God is speaking. For the sake of clarification and training we have added these three dimensions—*External, Internal* and *Mystical*—which describe the *location* from where you are receiving spiritual information. These dimensional sub-groups can be easily categorized as the following:

- **External** — Spiritual information revealed through the external, natural realm such as creation and the physical world around us.

- **Internal** — Spiritual information revealed through our internal realm as in our inner man, including our mind, will, and emotions.
- **Mystical** — Spiritual information revealed to our physical senses from the heavenly realm, including tangible experiences with the spirit realm, spiritual beings, etc.

Now, while the terms 'External' and 'Internal' are somewhat self-explanatory and generally acceptable, the term 'Mystical' can be somewhat offensive particularly to the Christian worldview, and understandably so. For centuries the word has evolved to include various meanings that are contrary to our Christian belief. However, I'd like to propose that the original greek meaning of the word was more in line with Scripture than opposed to it. The word 'mystical' was derived from the greek word *mysterion* or our English translation, 'mystery.' The root word connected to both mystical and mystery is *muo* which means *'to conceal.'* Biblically the term 'mystery' is frequently used when God has chosen to reveal what was once concealed.[7] Merriam-Webster defines the term *mystical* as *"having a spiritual meaning or reality that is neither apparent to the senses nor obvious to the intelligence; involving or having the nature of an individual's direct subjective communion with God."* [8] These definitions collectively speak to the truth that humans connect with spiritual realities that are not directly related to anything in the external or internal realm. This will become clearer as you read each of the following chapters and understand the different realms God speaks through. For now and the intent purposes of this book, the term *mystical* is fitting to describe the wonder and mystery of communicating with God in the spirit realm.

As you discover your hardwired ability to connect with God, it's important to understand that *all* receptors are spiritual receptors. None are more spiritual than the others. Your ability to hear God through the physical creation around you does not somehow qualify as a lesser spiritual experience than encountering an angelic being from Heaven. Both are accessing God's voice through your hearing receptor, however, *where* you recognize His voice coming from is distinctive. Hearing God in creation would be considered external hearing while hearing a message from Him through an angel that is speaking to you is mystical hearing. Each receptor is spiritual, and hearing God speak to us is always to be acknowledged and celebrated, no matter what "realm" through which you hear Him speak.

It can be tempting for us as humans to place more weight on hearing God in the mystical realm as a more elevated spiritual state. I see so many people minimize their own access to

---

7    Colossians 1:26-27, Mark 4:11, Romans 16:25

8    https://www.merriam-webster.com/dictionary/mystical

God's voice because they receive more in the natural realm and not what they deem as a spiritually superior realm. We don't mature by attaining levels of receptors that are seemingly more spiritual. We mature by growing to the full measure of Christ that is available to every single one of us.[9] Hearing God is not an academic achievement where we receive a PhD when we've successfully learned to access and activate every receptor possible. Hearing and knowing God is about relationally connecting to the Lord and positioning ourselves to hear Him in whatever way He is speaking.

Each of us can advance our maturity process by valuing and validating *every* receptor that God is speaking through. Knowing and clarifying these three sub-groups and how they relate to seeing, hearing, feeling, and perceiving God will expand your confidence in recognizing His voice.

---

9    Ephesians 4:13

## CHAPTER 2

## ALL-ACCESS PASS

Y OU ARE CREATED to live in unbroken communion with God. You are actually designed with the ability to see, hear, feel, and perceive Him. There is nothing about God that He does not want you to have access to. He has made it all possible. Yet, even knowing this to be true, have you ever felt that the odds of you hearing God speak can sometimes feel like winning the lottery?

When I was a young adult, there was a massive California lottery that continued to accumulate day by day. There were no winners for a long period of time, and the jackpot grew to an astronomically large amount of money so that even people who had never purchased a lottery ticket before went out and bought tickets. And, why not? Someone had to win that jackpot! Even I drank the lottery Kool-Aid and purchased a couple of tickets thinking, *"What if it's MY number that is called? I hope I win the jackpot!"* Needless to say, that didn't pay off.

Sometimes hearing God's voice can feel like that. It's like you're waiting and hoping that your lucky number will be chosen, and God will suddenly show up and speak to you. I think subconsciously there can be a belief that God is distant or far-off and maybe...perhaps...someday...He'll come meet me on a whim when it's not inconvenient for Him. That doesn't sound very constant or sure, but many live their spiritual lives with that mistaken mindset. Can I just encourage you that nothing could be further from the truth! We have been given an all-access pass to the heart of the Limitless One. God *wants* you to know Him as He knows you, and He has done everything possible on His end to make that a reality for us! He is God *near*. He is God *here*. He is God *in* us. We just need to learn to "pick up the phone" when He is calling and learn to recognize His voice.

Unfortunately, sometimes we like to make things more difficult for ourselves than is necessary. Salvation is a great example of this. God did all the upfront, hard work on our behalf. God gave His only beloved Son to a world that despised Him. Jesus had to endure torment, to die, and then to be resurrected from the grave while our part is to just say yes. Jesus did all the heavy lifting, and we got the gold medal. We only need to accept the gift of salvation that He freely gives in order to get the full benefits of salvation, freedom, and life.

Hearing His voice is the same. It's as easy as accepting a gift. It's as simple and natural as breathing. You may be asking the question, "*If it's so simple, why can't I hear God on a particular subject?*" Or perhaps you feel you've never really heard Him speak to you at all? I completely understand. The timing of certain answers may not always be when we want, but I guarantee you He *is* speaking, and the goal of this book is to accelerate and activate that revelation for you.

I love what Graham Cooke says: "*When you do by intention what you've done by intuition, you achieve acceleration.*" I believe you are already *intuitively* hearing from God. There may be some areas where you aren't aware that it is God speaking, but when the light switch is flipped on and you have those 'aha!'

moments, you will know without a doubt that *this* is the voice of God speaking to you! Once you know how you intuitively receive His voice, you can begin to intentionally practice recognizing His voice in that area more regularly. As a result, there will be an acceleration of consistent dialogue with the One who loves you best.

Before we move forward with the practical aspects of recognizing God speaking, let's lay down some biblical foundations of hearing God's voice that will strengthen your own communion with Him.

## *Foundation #1: Every person is hardwired.*

Every human being is hardwired to see, hear, feel and perceive spiritual information and possesses the capacity to discern God's voice. We find a key to this principle in the first letter to the Corinthians where the apostle Paul writes, *The spiritual did not come first, but the natural, and after that the spiritual.*[10] In context, he is talking about resurrection, but he is also laying the groundwork for a new kingdom mindset. Essentially, he is teaching that we can know what God is doing in the spiritual realm by looking at how He has patterned the natural one. Natural things reveal spiritual realities.

The story of creation is a good example. After God formed Adam's physical body, He *breathed* the breath of life into Adam. God's spiritual breath into Adam's physical body allowed mankind to come to life on earth. The gospel of John provides a spiritual parallel to this natural principle where we see Jesus breathing on His disciples and releasing the Holy Spirit

---

10    I Corinthians 15:46

on them.[11] Both occurrences of breath produced life—first in the natural and second in the spirit. God gave us the physical breath of life at Creation, and Jesus released the breath of His Spirit, bringing life to our spirit.

This principle applies to our topic because just as we are created in the natural to see, hear, feel, and perceive with our physical being, we are also created to see, hear, feel, and perceive spiritually. Your ability to communicate with God is as natural as your ability to breathe. You are made to do this. Since *all* of mankind is created in God's image,[12] every human being—believers and pre-Christians alike—have the innate potential for spiritual experiences and encounters because we are all hardwired to do so.

## *Foundation #2: Receptors are not exclusive.*

In my travels around the world as a trainer, I have observed too many people who disqualify themselves from receiving or recognizing God's voice because they believed seeing and hearing was a particular spiritual gift from God that was given to only a select few. The thought process goes something like this: *If I'm not hearing or seeing God like that person is, then I must not have the same ability or gift to see or hear God.*

Because many teachers and speakers have referred to people as having a spiritual "seeing gift" or "hearing gift," many conclude that they don't see or hear from God at all in those unique access points. That kind of language creates an exclusivity that couldn't be farther from the truth. Additionally, if you believe

---

11   John 20:22

12   Genesis 1:27

seeing or hearing God is actually a *spiritual gift* for the select few, then you might invalidate or nullify all of the ways He is *already speaking* to you. Seeing, hearing, sensing, and perceiving are not gifts of the Spirit. Obviously, everything in life is a gift from God—from the air we breathe to our health, home, families, and everything we see around us. I am not referring here to the universal gifts that God gives all of us but rather to the specific spiritual gifts as laid out in scripture.

Biblically, various spiritual gifts are given to different people according to the measure of grace allotted to them.[13] Spiritual gifts like prophecy, wisdom, hospitality, revelation, and helps are all examples of valuable gifts given to encourage and strengthen the Body of Christ.[14] However, our receptors of seeing, hearing, sensing and perceiving are not included in the list of spiritual gifts for the sake of building up the Church in scriptures because we are all already hardwired with these receptors. This is an important distinction here as I believe it will help set some free from believing they've been disqualified or excluded from receiving from God in these areas.

### Foundation #3: Believers have the ability to recognize His voice.

Many pre-Christians today are hearing God's voice because they are hardwired to do so. They just don't know that it's *Him* speaking. Out of ignorance, they attribute the information they are receiving to themselves, "mother earth," or any other spiritual or natural substitute. The primary difference for believers

---

13    Ephesians 4:7

14    I Corinthians 12

is that we have a relationship with the Lord Jesus Christ, and when He speaks, we can recognize His voice more easily than those who don't know Him personally. That is the power of His Spirit in you.

Just as every believer has full access to the voice of God, it is also their responsibility to judge and discern His voice. Scriptures tell us that God is speaking in multiple ways.

> *For God does speak—now one way, now another—*
> *though no one perceives it.*
>
> *Job 33:14*

It is our responsibility to perceive not only what He is speaking but *how* He is speaking. The ancient writings of Job reveal that God speaks in multiple ways—*now one way, now another—*but that it is equally the responsibility of the receiver to perceive what He is saying. This was one of the purposes for the writing of this book, to help you identify how He is already speaking to you as well as expand your ability to discern and perceive His voice in whichever way He chooses to speak.

The book of Proverbs says it like this: *"So train your heart to listen when I speak."*[15] It is *our* responsibility to train our hearts to listen when He speaks, not God's. In the gospel of John, Jesus reveals a characteristic of those that belong to Him. He says, *"My sheep listen to my voice; I know them, and they follow me."*[16] God would never hold us accountable for something we could not legitimately fulfill. How could we follow Him if we didn't have the capacity to know and recognize His voice? The truth

---

15 Proverbs 2:2 Passion Translation

16 John 10:27-30

is we are all hardwired to hear and receive from God, and the evidence is found within our human design.

## Foundation #4: We are hardwired to respond.

It is our responsibility to learn to not only recognize but also respond to God's voice, and we do this when we practice intentionality. We are active and not passive. Let me explain what that looks like practically in the life of Israel's great deliverer, Moses.

In the book of Exodus, we find Moses, the exiled prince of Egypt living in Midian after murdering an Egyptian and losing favor with both Pharaoh and the Israelites. Look at what happens when God catches Moses' eyes with something strange. We pick up his story in the third chapter of Exodus:

> *Now Moses was tending the flock of Jethro, his father-in-law, the priest of Midian, and he led the flock to the far side of the wilderness and came to Horeb, the mountain of God. There the angel of the Lord appeared to him in flames of fire from within a bush. Moses saw that though the bush was on fire it did not burn up. So, Moses thought, 'I will go over and see this strange sight—why the bush does not burn up.'*
>
> *Exodus 3:1-3*

Moses had just been going about his daily routine, tending his father-in-law's sheep. I'm sure he had seen many burning bushes in his career as a shepherd in the wilderness, but there was something unique about this particular bush. Moses saw something that caught his eye, and then he responded by *turning aside* to see. This is the point for us that I want you to catch: Moses went from *passively* seeing to *actively* looking when he took an action step. He turned aside; he went over to get a closer look at the bush to understand what was happening. As a result, when the Lord saw that Moses had turned aside, an encounter was initiated that would forever alter Moses' life and would set him on a path to become the future deliverer of Israel and God's friend. Notice that it was only *when* Moses turned aside to see that the Lord gave Moses his mission. This is the power of looking to see with intentionality.

I believe there are "burning bushes" all around us every day. God has already initiated an invitation through our natural surroundings to turn aside and draw closer to Him. It's up to us to respond to His voice by adjusting our attention through active looking, hearing, seeing, and perceiving. Let's not miss divine opportunities by passively engaging with what's around us. We can activate all of our receptors by making the daily choice to be intentional in our response to what He is saying.

# CHAPTER 3

## EXTERNAL SEEING

*God speaking through what we see*
*in the Natural, Created Realm*

E VERY PERSON IS CREATED to see. Seeing is connected to our eyes—both natural and spiritual, literal and figurative. Some see the glories of the Lord in the natural creation around us. Others see God in visions and dreams and in their imaginations while some even peer through the heavenly veil to witness the mysteries of the spirit realm. As mentioned previously, one of the primary keys to activating any of your receptors is to practice intentionality versus passivity.

> *I will stand at my watch and station myself on the ram-*
> *parts; I will **look to see** what he will say to me, and what*
> *answer I am to give to this complaint.*
>
> *Hab. 2:1*

The prophet Habakkuk gives us a powerful tool to actively stir up our perception of seeing. Notice that Habbakuk was not just stationing himself and casually seeing what was around him. No, he was fixed, feet firmly planted and positioned while his eyes focused on what was inevitably coming—the word of the Lord.

In the context of our seeing receptors, there is a difference between looking and seeing, and it's more than just a play on words. Looking to see carries a greater responsibility and is active while the static state of seeing without paying attention is passive. We often *see* passively, but *looking to see* requires intention and action. For example, when you are driving a car, you are passively seeing the landscape as you speed by, but you should also be actively looking to see the road in front of you. Looking to see is essentially a matter of what you choose to focus your attention on.

With this principle of active looking, let's explore further the concept of seeing spiritually through the external or natural realm. In the first chapter of Paul's letter to the Romans, we find a primary key to discerning God's voice in and through creation.

> *For since the creation of the world God's invisible qualities—His eternal power and divine nature—**have been clearly seen, being understood from what has been made,** so that people are without excuse.*
>
> *Romans 1:20*

The temporal world around us reveals eternal truths about Christ in us. Everything we see—nature, animals, plants, people, the stars, the universe—*every created thing* reveals truths about the nature and character of God. Everything we see has God's "fingerprint" on it, His DNA so-to-speak. What we see in creation becomes an invitation into divine dialogue. In fact,

God takes it a step further in this passage and tells us that we have no excuse if we *don't* see Him in His creation! It's actually our responsibility to intentionally look for His divine attributes in the created realm around us.

God is initiating encounters with us through what we *see*, and I believe He is inviting us into a conversation more often than we are recognizing it. We are captivated by the beauty and grandeur of creation but have failed to discern its message. This fact is evidenced by how many songs, poems, and art pieces have been dedicated to creation. Many of you reading this book right now have photos on your phone or camera of something that caught your eye in the natural. Perhaps you were moved by a stunning vibrant sunset or the many hues of color found in spring flowers. Maybe it was the joy on a child's face as they were riding their new bike for the first time. When we learn to look for who God is in what we see, we will grow in understanding His voice speaking through the world around us. Seeing spiritually like this in the natural realm is a valid dimension of seeing, and it comes from our commitment to seek what God is saying.

God spoke to Jeremiah through what he saw. Look at the following passage and notice how the word of the Lord came to the ancient prophet through what he saw externally.

> *This is the word that came to Jeremiah from the Lord: 'Go down to the potter's house, and there I will give you my message.' So I went down to the potter's house, and I **saw him working at the wheel**. But the pot he was shaping from the clay was marred in his hands; so the potter formed it into another pot, shaping it as seemed best to him.*
>
> *Then the word of the Lord came to me. He said, 'Can I not do with you, Israel, as this potter does?' declares the Lord.*

*'Like clay in the hand of the potter, so are you in my hand, Israel.'*

*Jeremiah 18:1-6*

God spoke a powerful message about the nation of Israel through something Jeremiah physically saw. The key we learn from Jeremiah is that he was intently looking and expectant that God would speak through what he saw at the potter's house, and we can do the same.

We've all heard the phrase, a *picture is worth a thousand words*, and it's true. Often, more can be spoken through a visual image than what words can convey. When we understand that God truly speaks through what we see in the external created realm, the thing that we see can become the messenger for what God is communicating. Now let's explore some specific ways we can see God speak to us through the external, natural realm around us.

## Creation

We can see God speaking through what He created because creation has its own voice. Just as we saw in the first chapter of Romans that we have no excuse if we don't recognize God's divine attributes in creation, creation itself is speaking and revealing its own knowledge of God.

*The heavens declare the glory of God;*
*The skies proclaim the work of His hands.*
*Day after day they pour forth speech;*
*Night after night they reveal knowledge.*
*They have no speech; they use no words;*
*No sound is heard from them.*

*Yet their voice goes out into all the earth,*
*And their words to the ends of the world.*

*Psalm 19:1-4*

Creation has its own revelation of God, and God speaks to us through what He has made. Here is another example from the life of Jeremiah where God spoke a powerful word about the nation of Israel through something Jeremiah saw in nature.

*The word of the Lord came to me: 'What do you see, Jeremiah?' '**I see the branch of an almond tree,**' I replied. The Lord said to me, "You have seen correctly, for I am watching to see that my word is fulfilled.'*

*Jeremiah 1:11,12*

Ok, catch this. The only object that Jeremiah saw was a branch of a tree. Yet, he was commended by the Lord for seeing correctly! How many of us have gazed in awe at the limitless expanse of the ocean or the majesty of the mountains not realizing that God was speaking to us through what He has created? The book of Proverbs instructs us *to go to the ant* where we can learn from its wisdom in how to store up provisions. The book of Matthew exhorts us to *consider the birds of the air and the lilies of the field* so that we would put our unfailing trust in His ability and desire to take care of us, just as He takes care of them. I don't know about you, but when I see a bunch of ants in my house, I usually look for the bug spray rather than looking for what God may be trying to communicate. The point is God is *already speaking* through creation and nature around us. Our responsibility is to pay attention to what He is saying through what we are seeing and respond accordingly.

27

Years ago, I was sitting outside of our local coffee shop, soaking up the sun, and enjoying some family conversations with my mom and sister. As we were talking, a hummingbird suddenly flew near us and started to fly around us. We were all admiring the beautiful little bird when the hummingbird shocked us all and landed on my mother's lap where it stayed still for a full minute. Then as suddenly as it landed, it burst back to life and took off flying away. Because it was so unusual for a hummingbird to do something like that, we were all intrigued by the interaction with the small creature and started to *look to see* what the Lord could be speaking through it. To us, a hummingbird represented resurrection life and healing displayed through its ability to seemingly 'come back to life' after having been asleep or still. Within days of that encounter, my mom went into a season where she was diagnosed with both cancer and a stroke almost simultaneously. It was not a pleasant time for her, but she came through strong and healthy. It was comforting to know that God had already spoken His promise of life to her through that little hummingbird.

Below are two documented stories of animals interacting and supernaturally protecting people:

> *In June 2005, a twelve-year-old girl was snatched by four men in rural south-west Ethiopia as she made her way home from school. A week after the kidnapping, her captors were attempting to move her with police in hot pursuit when three lions chased the men off. The lions remained with the terrified girl until police officers arrived to escort her to safety. She told them that although she had been beaten by her kidnappers – who it is believed had been attempting to sell her into a forced marriage – the lions had not touched her.*

*Sergeant Wondmu Wedaj said, 'They stood guard until we found her and then they just left her like a gift and went back into the forest. Everyone thinks this is some kind of miracle because normally the lions would attack people.'*

---

*Rheal Guindon, a young boy in Ontario, Canada, was out on a camping trip with his parents when they decided to go fishing. Rheal stayed onshore but was appalled to witness his parents' boat tip over and his parents tragically drown. Panic-stricken, he attempted to walk to the nearest town to get help, but as the sun set, he realized he would have to spend the night outside.*

*As he lay on the ground, traumatized by this ordeal, he felt 'a warm, furry body' press up against him. Thinking it was a dog, he fell asleep. On waking up the next morning, he found three wild beavers snuggled up against him. They had saved him from freezing to death overnight when temperatures had dipped below zero.[17]*

Recognizing God's voice to us is not just the words that are being communicated but His heart and character as well. God sent ravens to bring food to the prophet Elijah by the brook.[18] Is it beyond the scope of imagination that the Lord would send three beavers to protect a small child, keeping him warm from the harsh winter elements? All of these stories reveal the astounding love and protection of the Father through creation around us.

---

17   https://www.onegreenplanet.org/animalsandnature/stories-of-amazing-times-wild-animals-saved-people-in-need/

18   I Kings 17:6

George Washington Carver, the innovative scientist who discovered over 300 uses for the peanut, said this regarding God's voice in nature. *"I love to think of nature as an unlimited broadcasting station through which God speaks to us every hour if we will only tune in."* [19] God speaks through what you see in creation around you. What is He saying to you today?

## *Objects, Colors and Clothing*

Seeing isn't difficult. You're already doing it, but perhaps you haven't learned the spiritual tools to interact with what you're seeing. Remember, we are all hardwired to see spiritually what God is saying in the natural realm. It is as simple as paying attention or like Moses, turning aside to see through those things that catch our eye. Many people can believe that God would speak through His creation, but do they believe that He can speak through all created things? I have seen the Lord speak through colors, clothing, jewelry, objects in the room, gifts, nature—you name it! Everyday household items and natural objects don't sound particularly spiritual, yet, the Lord highlighted an almond branch and a boiling pot to speak a message to Israel through His servant, Jeremiah.[20] Man's creation can also be the messenger of God's voice. For those who intentionally fix their eyes to see what the Lord is speaking in the natural world, there are life-changing messages to be heard.

Years ago, I was part of a team that was ministering at a conference in England. As part of the ministry team, our job was to look for those we felt the Lord was 'highlighting' to us and then

19    https://www.inspiringquotes.us/author/4029-george-washington -carver
20    Jeremiah 1:11-14

speak an encouraging word to them. My eye was drawn to an African couple who were both wearing clothing with varying shades of deep purple and royal blue. Often the clothing people wear is an expression of their personality, preferences, and identity. When I saw the colors they were wearing, it immediately made me think of "royalty" as I associate those colors with nobility and authority.

As I was contemplating this, I had an internal dialogue with the Lord about it. *Lord, I can't just tell them that they are royalty because technically we are ALL royalty. We all are Your sons and daughters, and, honestly, the whole 'royalty' word just seems so overused right now. It feels like a Christian buzzword even though it may be true. Can you speak to me about something more significant for this couple?*

After dialoguing further with the Lord, the impression of this couple's royal status would not leave me, so I shared with them the encouraging picture I had for them. I encouraged them first that, even though we all are technically royalty as children of the King, that they *really were* royalty, and that God sees them that way.

When the meeting was over, the man came forward and gave me some feedback on how the word had impacted his wife and him. Apparently, he was the former ambassador and advisor to an African king. The man was accustomed to being in the presence of royalty but had recently been exiled due to a coup in their nation. Privately, he had been asking the Lord if he would ever serve in that royal capacity again, and the Lord had confirmed he would through the encouragement I had given to him. Then, he proceeded to tell me that his wife was actually the daughter of the African king. She was, in fact, a princess, literal royalty. This African couple was incredibly encouraged and felt strengthened to continue in their journey because they had felt known and seen by God.

This testimony is amazing, but my point here is to notice how the process of receiving God's voice unfolded. First, I saw the color purple. Then, the colors of ordinary clothes they were wearing caught my eye, and I 'turned aside' to ask the Lord what it might mean. It was as simple as that. God speaking to us can be as simple as paying attention to the things that catch our eyes.

A pastor once told a friend of mine that God spoke to him through people's jewelry. My friend was quite skeptical at first, but he asked the pastor to show him what he meant. My friend had recently been given a Citizen-brand watch called a *Blue Angel*. The watch is popular among pilots because it features different time zones from around the world. The pastor looked at my friend's watch and shared an encouraging word that the Lord would soon be opening ministry opportunities to him all around the world. Within one year, global invitations poured in, and my friend found himself flying all over the globe. That encouraging word from God came by the pastor observing my friend's watch and asking God what He was speaking through it. God loves to use simple practical things to share deep spiritual truths.

## *Scripture*

One of the most obvious and powerful ways to *see* what God is saying is to read His Word. Psalm 119:105 states, "*Your word is a lamp for my feet and a light on my path.*"

Have you ever read the Bible only to have a scripture "jump" out at you or maybe seem '"highlighted" in the moment? This is often God *speaking* to you through what you are *seeing* in His word. Reading and studying the Bible is one of my favorite ways of seeing God speak to me.

Years ago, when I was in college, I was working at a bank as a teller. I had only been working at this bank for about three months, but already I was experiencing a difficult time with my direct manager. She had a reputation of being a very challenging person, lacking people and managerial skills. The work environment became so stressful and toxic that one morning before I went into work, I asked the Lord to speak to me about what to do in this volatile situation. I closed my eyes and opened my bible to a random page to see what my eyes would land on—sort of like "Bible roulette." Although I don't recommend this method for regular daily reading and meditation, honestly, there have been a few significant times that God has spoken to me this way in the past.

Once my finger landed on the page, I opened my eyes and immediately saw Proverbs 10:22, *"The blessing of the Lord brings wealth, without painful toil to it."* My heart leapt within me because I knew I had my answer! I didn't know how God was going to do it yet, but I believed that His heart was to bless me and that it was not His will to bring toil or sorrow to His blessing. I walked in to work that morning full of hope like I hadn't felt in weeks, knowing that God had spoken to me.

As soon as I arrived at the bank, my irritable manager called me over and proceeded to tell me that I wasn't a right "fit" for the job, and they were letting me go. What? That wasn't the answer I was expecting at all! And yet, immediately I felt so much relief and freedom and knew it was God's will. Shortly after, I applied for a job at a credit union where I worked for almost four years and had incredible favor with the job, customers, and fellow co-workers. God's blessings carry with it peace, and there is no striving and sorrow attached to it. God speaks through the written word of Scripture.

## *Numbers*

I wanted to mention how God can speak through numbers briefly in this section of external seeing. Numbers are a large part of God's voice throughout the scripture. I am not referring to a human or earthly system of numerology, which tries to predict futures with numbers outside of a relationship with God. That dependence of numbers is a distortion of God's original intent and design. However, knowing that God speaks through *all* of creation, we cannot limit his voice to only those things we approve of or feel comfortable with.

Throughout the Bible and creation, we see patterns of numbers that represent a specific message from God for those who look to see like the message of Daniel's seventy-sevens[21] or Pharaoh's seven years of plenty and seven years of lack.[22] As we have already discovered, God loves to bring revelation to those who will search it out.[23] Let me share a personal story of how the Lord spoke to me using numbers.

Many years ago, my family was looking to purchase our first home. This had been a long-awaited promise from the Lord to me personally, and we finally had enough money saved up for a down payment. Because of our budget, we had looked at one house that was nice and checked some of the boxes of what we

---

21  Daniel 9:24-27

22  Genesis 41

23  Proverbs 25:2

were wanting, but we didn't have a full peace about it yet. There was also another house I had my eye on, but it was an additional two hundred thousand dollars, which was a stretch for what we thought we could financially afford at the time. Still, because of the uniqueness of the property, we decided to at least take a look at it.

When we arrived at the property, it felt like I was home. The house sat on an incredibly beautiful, 13-acre park-like setting with everything we had desired and more. There was only one minor issue: the price. Now, because of my personal relationship with the Lord, I had no problem whatsoever stepping out in faith and purchasing this house if this was what the Lord was wanting to give us. However, I knew we needed to hear His voice clearly to make that step.

As I was praying and asking the Lord, my eye was drawn to the address of the house. I felt like there was something the Lord wanted to speak to me through that number and began asking Him about it. I felt drawn to look up its meaning in the *Hebrew Lexicon*, something I don't normally do with numbers. As I was flipping towards 226 in my concordance, I asked the Lord, *I just need a sign from you that this is the house You have for us. Please, just give us a sign.* When I flipped to the number in the Hebrew concordance, this was the definition of that word: *A sign, a distinguishing mark, a miraculous sign.* Wow! I had asked God for a sign and the number of the home address literally meant a *miraculous sign* in the Hebrew concordance. We had our answer! We purchased that house, and it has been an incredible blessing to our family for many years now.

Speaking through numbers is just one example of the many ways God can speak. Pursue His voice. Seek out a greater understanding in the ways that He is speaking, and you will be blessed. Activating your ability to see spiritually in the natural realm begins with paying attention to those initial items that catch your eye. Instead of dismissing the items in the moment, pause and ask the Lord if it means something. Begin dialoguing with Him about what you are seeing. There is a wealth of knowledge hidden in creation that is available to those who are looking to see His voice in the external world around us.

# CHAPTER 4

## INTERNAL SEEING

*Seeing God speak through the Internal Realm*

F ROM THE FOUNDATIONS of creation, God's original design is that we would be like Him; we are created in His image.

> *So God **created mankind in His own image**, in the image of God He created them; male and female He created them.*
>
> Genesis 1:27

You are hardwired to see spiritually just as God sees through the internal realm of imaginations, dreams, and visions. God saw an image of you in His imagination before any life was formed. From that internal picture, He called you forth into existence to live in this time and generation. God created *you* from His imagination.[24] Your imagination is an integral part of your born-again nature, and it's an important receptor in

---

24  Jeremiah 1:5

connecting with and receiving from God. The imagination is the foundation for plans and ideas. It is the seat where concepts, purpose, and the intellectual structure is formed, much like a potter forms the clay. How many of you have ever had a good idea just spontaneously "drop" into your mind? Or perhaps a solution or strategy to accomplish something involuntarily appeared in your imagination? Have you recognized that this is potentially one of the ways God speaks to you?

The truth is everything you physically see around you at one point was inside of someone's imagination—whether God's or man's. It's been said that *imagination is the greatest nation in the world,*[25] and I have to agree as some of the greatest inventions and creations on earth have come from God-inspired imagination. Electricity, cars, planes, medicine, design, architecture—everything created in this world by God or man ultimately began with an internal vision. The creation took seed form as an internal picture or image of what *could be* and eventually was manifested into our physical reality through intentional action. The internal became the external.

According to Webster's Dictionary definition, imagination *allows us to see what has never been perceived in reality.* For example, right now if you closed your eyes and were asked to picture a pink elephant, how many of you could see a pink elephant in your mind's eye? How about a crocodile with rabbit ears? Both of these seem nonsensical as no one has actually seen a living pink elephant or a bunny-eared crocodile because they don't exist in our physical world. And yet, I can "see" it. That's the power of imagination. This power to create in our mind allows us to see what was previously impossible, and

---

25   Bob Proctor

as new creations in Christ through partnership with the Holy Spirit, we use this powerful receptor to see what God is saying. Imagination as a form of seeing with your mind, reminds me of a scripture in Isaiah:

> *"You will keep him in perfect peace, whose **mind** is stayed on You, because he trusts in You."*
>
> Isaiah 26:3

The word "mind" in the above passage is not the usual Hebrew word used for the mind or thoughts of man. Its root literally means *creative imagination.*[26] Simply put, we could say that he whose creative imagination is firmly fixed on the Lord will enjoy perfect peace, health, happiness, and well-being.

As a side note, although imaginations must be judged just like any other vision or impression you believe is from God, they should not automatically be rejected. Scripture tells us that as born-again believers, we now have the mind of Christ.[27] His mind includes His imagination which means that our imagination can now be a great and expansive source of receiving divine information and communing with Him. As we learn to test and trust a sanctified imagination, it can accelerate our own ability to see in the Spirit. Scripture tells us that we can't even begin to *imagine* what God has prepared for us!

> *What no eye has seen, what no ear has heard, and what **no human mind has conceived (imagined)**—*

---

26   https://www.blueletterbible.org/lang/lexicon/lexicon.cfm?Strongs=H3336&t=NASB95

27   I Corinthians 2:16

*the things God has prepared for those who love Him* — these are the things God has prepared for those who love him."

I Corinthians 2:9

Therefore, we must create a higher value for inner imaginations and impressions. Many of us have been taught not to focus on our daydreams or imaginations. Perhaps you've been told it is a waste of time to daydream or that your imagination is corrupt due to your old sin nature. Believers can often be afraid of being misled by their imaginations, but God wants to teach us to harness the power of a *sanctified* imagination to see what He is saying. It is time to undo those lies that our imaginations are evil and trust that God has given you a sanctified imagination in Christ. As my friend and colleague Dan McCollam says, *"When you gave your whole life to Christ, He took it all — spirit, soul and body!"* Jesus didn't take just a part but the whole of you. So, trust as you yield your heart and imaginations to Him that He is speaking.

Now let's explore some of the ways that we receive revelation and information from God through our internal seeing receptors.

## *Pictures and Images*

God also speaks through pictures and images that come to our mind as internal imaginations. When receiving from God in this way, these mental pictures often come spontaneously under the inspiration of the Spirit. Jesus himself heard God speak to him in this way.

> *Nathanael said to Him, 'How do you know me?' Jesus answered and said to him, 'Before Philip called you, when you were under the fig tree, I **saw** you.*
>
> John 1:48

Jesus *had seen* Nathanael sitting under the fig tree. He didn't see Nathanael with his physical eyes but rather with his internal sight. God spoke to Jesus by showing him an image of Nathanael in his mind's eye. Inspired pictures and images are one of the ways God speaks to us and what we see in the person of Jesus is available to us.

Many years ago, we needed a new car for our growing family, so we drove the four-hour commute down from the mountains to the Los Angeles area to see if we could find something. By the time we arrived, it was already late in the evening. Although all of the car lots were closed, we decided to drive to the nearest auto mall and walk around so we could get a head start on what options were available to us. On the long drive to the auto mall, I saw a mental image of a black Honda Pilot with tinted windows, a roof rack, and running boards. Because of this visual image in my mind's eye along with a particular purchase price, we had a potential target and set off for a walk around the car lots to see if we could locate what I was "seeing"— kind of like a treasure hunt.

By the end of our hour-long walk and after looking at hundreds of cars, there was only one car that stood out. It was as if the sky parted and a ray of light shone down from heaven. What we saw was a black Honda Pilot with tinted windows, a roof rack, and running boards—exactly what I had seen in my imagination, and the price point was right at our budget. The next morning, we went back to the dealer and purchased the car with confidence, knowing God had revealed to us His heart and goodness. To this day, it was the best family car we had ever owned.

This may seem a trivial thing to some that God would even care to speak about which car to buy, and I've bought many reliable cars where I didn't have an internal picture of what it should look like. However, I believe with my whole heart if it matters to me, it matters to God. He cares about the things we care about, and He loves to be invited into our process. I'm not saying that we have to ask God what car to buy every time we need one— He's our Father, not our micro-manager—but He loves to see the choices we make when we learn to delight ourselves in Him.

Another time when God surprised me with an internal picture was at a women's conference in Northern California. During the worship preceding a main session, I saw a picture in my imagination of a poppy field. Within this field of flowers, there was one poppy that was taller than the rest, and it was opening itself up towards the sun. The scripture out of Isaiah came to me, *Arise, shine for your light has come.*[28] The picture was so vivid to me, that I picked up my pencil and drew a rough sketch in my journal to try and capture it.

When worship was over, we sat down to listen to the speaker. During the entire session, the speaker was releasing a grace for the women in the room to champion other people's time to shine. As she closed her session, she put up a PowerPoint picture. It was a photograph of a poppy field where one poppy was higher than the rest and was facing up to the sun—the exact image of the picture the Lord showed me during worship. God was speaking through the internal

---

28    Isaiah 60:1

picture He had given me and confirming His word through the speaker that it was time for me to rise up and shine in the area He had called me.

In September of 2019, a friend of mine had an internal picture of the entire world wearing face masks. She interpreted this from the Lord as something that was coming and proceeded to tell her husband and her friend that they should start a mask-production company based on the image she saw. Both her husband and her friend talked her out of it.

Six months later, the world-wide COVID pandemic hit and like her picture, the entire world was suddenly wearing masks. If she had started a mask company, she would have been prepared in advance to help many, especially during the initial stages of the pandemic when masks were in short supply. Though there is so much grace when we miss it, it is important that we pay greater attention to these unsolicited inspired pictures and images to see if God is speaking through them.

## *Dreams and Visions of the Night*

*In a dream, in a vision of the night, when deep sleep falls on people as they slumber in their beds, he may speak in their ears...*
*Job 33:15-16a*

There are twenty-one dreams recorded in the scriptures with the majority of them taking place in the books of Genesis and Matthew. God communicated various messages in these dreams, including warnings, destinies, and direction. Dreams and visions of the night were a prominent and powerful way for God to speak to many people in the Bible, and it's an important and valid way that He still speaks today. Look at God's promise given by the prophet Joel that was fulfilled on the day of Pentecost.

> *In the last days, God says,*
> *I will pour out my Spirit on all people.*
> *Your sons and daughters will prophesy,*
> **Your young men will see visions,**
> **Your old men will dream dreams.**
>
> *Acts 2:17-18*

Most people who believe that they do not see in the Spirit are merely not recognizing all the ways that God speaks. They think the identifiers of "seeing in the Spirit" only belong to those who go into heavenly trances or interact with the angelic realm like the apostle Paul and John the Revelator did. But dreams are an important part of the great outpouring package that was delivered on the day of Pentecost, and the realm of internal sight, including dreams, can be a credible source for hearing from God.

One day when my oldest daughter, Faith, was about twelve, I was taking her to her soccer game early for warm-ups. She was a skilled soccer player, and it was always a joy to watch her play the position of forward on the team. As I was driving, I suddenly remembered a dream I had had the night before about her. In my dream, the goalie for her team was sick and was unable to play. So, the coach decided to put Faith in the goalie's place even though she had never played goalie before. In the dream, her team was already short-handed on the field, and the opposing team had taken advantage of their lack of defense, making several goal attempts, striking towards the goal over and over. However, in my dream, Faith blocked every single goal, defending against about twenty to thirty goal attempts.

I shared my dream with Faith and dropped her off for pre-practice then ran home to take care of a few things before the game started. At half-time, I drove up, expecting to see Faith on the field in her usual position as forward. Instead, I saw her in the box, playing goalie. When she saw me walk up, she yelled across the field, *Mom! It's your dream!* The entire soccer game unfolded just as it had in my dream.

What was the purpose of the dream? Personally, I believe it was to give my daughter the courage she needed to step into and own her unexpected position as goalie. She was strengthened by the fact that God had already revealed this unforeseen circumstance and that His plan was to help her be successful where she otherwise might have been afraid. God speaks through our dreams, and He is revealing His heart and will.

I believe that God is already speaking to you through your dreams, and I want to encourage you to begin valuing the dreams you have. Maybe you're not much of a night dreamer, or perhaps you don't really remember your dreams. There are many incredible resources out there that will help activate this form of communing with the Lord that I highly recommend.[29] Thanksgiving is the gateway for multiplication, and when we thank the Lord for what He already has given us—in this case, our ability to dream—He opens the storehouses for more.

### Inner Visions

Another type of seeing internally is the realm of visions. Both dreams *and* visions were part of the great outpouring of

---

29 Doug Addison and John Paul Jacksn both have great resources on understanding dreams.

God's Spirit on mankind.[30] The greek definition of a *vision* is *mentally to perceive or see; a sight divinely granted in an ecstasy or in sleep.*[31] The major difference between visions and dreams is that visions happen while you are awake, conscious, or in a trance-like state while dreams happen when you are asleep. There are just as many biblical references to visions as there are to dreams. In fact, visions are mentioned more than one hundred times in the Bible and were experienced by persons in both the Old and New Testament as a valid way of God speaking to them. And guess what? He still speaks to us through visions today.

Practically, a vision looks like a series of pictures played out, almost like a movie to the viewer. Where an internal picture would be a single image, a vision is more like a short or long movie, all taking place in the theater of your imagination. Visions from God will often give direction, instruction, and contain messages about what to do as He did with Ananias.

> *In Damascus there was a disciple named Ananias. The Lord **called to him in a vision**, 'Ananias!' 'Yes, Lord,' he answered. The Lord told him, 'Go to the house of Judas....'*
> Acts 9:10-11

Most untrained people believe that visions either occur sovereignly, or they don't happen at all, at least, not to them. However, the truth is that visions increase when we learn to yield ourselves to the presence of the LORD. One of the most effective and powerful tools to increase your capacity for vision is to meditate on scripture. The next time you read a Bible story,

---

30   Acts 2

31   https://www.blueletterbible.org/lexicon/g3705/nasb20/mgnt/0-1/

practice picturing how the story plays out in your imagination. Dwelling on and contemplating the written word in this way can develop your capacity for spiritual vision.

Also, reflect on your own personal times with the Lord. In moments of deep prayer, worship, or intimacy with God watch for the unfolding of visions. How often has a picture come to mind when you were in the middle of praying for someone or a particular circumstance? Probably more than you realized. Learning that this is one of the ways God speaks to us will increase your ability to recognize and respond to His voice in these moments. What you focus on becomes magnified and just like pictures and dreams, an increased value for visions will cause them to increase in frequency and clarity.

A few years ago, I was asked to be part of a ministry team to pray and speak life over a young couple visiting from Russia. As we were praying, I saw a vision of the woman we were praying for in my imagination. I watched as she was powerfully speaking to an audience on a large platform, and the woman appeared bold and confident in what she was releasing. I shared this vision with her, and she began weeping. She said that the vision I had of her was the same image as a dream she has had since she was a little girl. The woman had been asking God that very day if her dream would ever come forth. The vision God showed me was a confirming and encouraging word to her that she was on track to fulfill her destiny.

Pictures, dreams, and visions are all part of the same outpouring of the Holy Spirit that was released on all flesh. In this chapter, you have learned the importance of dreams and visions as ways that a believer can internally see in the Spirit. As we develop a greater value for how God speaks in these ways, we can cultivate a stronger awareness and sensitivity to how God is already speaking to us through our capacity for internal seeing.

# Chapter 5

## Mystical Seeing

*Physically seeing the Spirit Realm*

W HEN YOU WERE A CHILD, do you ever remember being frightened by dark shadows in the bedroom? I do. I used to make sure my closet door was closed every night before I went to sleep because I was sure something sinister was lurking inside of it. Or perhaps, you were convinced that a monster was living under your bed? The normal attitude taken towards children experiencing this particular type of nighttime fear is to chalk it up to a vivid imagination. It is entirely plausible that children today are feeding too much on negative television programs, influencing their thought life, but it is also possible they are actually seeing with their physical eyes a spiritual reality.

For some, physically seeing into the spirit realm is extremely common and natural for them. From childhood, these individuals have been able to see with their natural eyes both angelic and demonic activity in some form or another. Often this ability is rooted in the biblical gift of discerning of spirits. Like all other receptors, one can earnestly desire, ask, and develop a greater awareness in this area.

In the first chapter, we studied how God trained His prophets by asking them what they saw. God asked Zechariah the same question he had asked Jeremiah: *"What do you see?"* However, Zechariah was not seeing something from the natural, created realm around him or even from the internal realm of pictures and imaginations. Zechariah saw with his natural eyes a spiritual reality. Look at the example below:

> *Then I lifted up my eyes again and looked and behold*
> *there was a flying scroll. And He said to me, 'What do you see?'*
> *I answered, 'I see a flying scroll,*
> *thirty feet long and fifteen feet wide.'*
>
> *Zechariah 5:2*

The fact that Zechariah *lifted his eyes* and looked indicates that he was receiving spiritual information through his mystical seeing receptors. Was he a prophet? Absolutely. Does God only speak in this mystical way to the special few? Scripturally, no. Though it may not seem as common a way to commune with God as some of the other receptors, it is nonetheless not exclusive. Remember, we are all created to connect with God in any way He is speaking. Let's look at some practical examples of this type of seeing in the Spirit.

## Angels

Throughout the Old and New Testament, we read stories of angels appearing to men and delivering messages from God, helping them, giving direction, and even warring on their behalf. In fact, from the very first three chapters of Genesis through the last chapter of Revelation, we see angels fulfilling God's will and interacting with men.

One of the most classic accounts of seeing angels in the spirit realm comes from the story of Elisha and his servant. The King of Aram had sent his army to capture Elisha. When his servant boy left the tent in the morning and saw that they were completely surrounded by their enemies, he panicked. But Elisha did not seem fazed or concerned for his safety at all. Why? Because he was seeing a superior reality; the servant boy was not.

> *And Elisha prayed, 'Open his eyes, LORD, so that he may see.' Then the LORD opened the servant's eyes, and he looked and saw the hills full of horses and chariots of fire all around Elisha.*
>
> 2 Kings 6:15

The servant boy's heart was strengthened, encouraged, and comforted by the revelation that there were more for them than those who were against them. In this example, we can assume that Elisha was already seeing mystically because when he prayed on his servant's behalf, he asked the Lord to open his (the servant boy) eyes. It was as if Elijah was saying, "Lord, let my servant see into the spirit realm with his physical eyes what I already see. Show him the true reality of this situation."

Growing up, I used to share a room with my younger sister. She recounts a story about when she was five years old and waking up in the middle of the night, seeing a brilliant angel standing at the foot of my bed, watching and guarding me. She was so afraid that she shut her eyes and put the covers over her face so she wouldn't see it. Fear seems to be a typical initial response to physical encounters with the angelic as shown in scriptures.[32]

Another time, my sister had woken up in the middle of the night and had a spontaneous thought to look out the bedroom window which was above her bed. She stood up and peered through the widow where she suddenly came face to face with an angel! These two events from childhood are forever imprinted into my sister's memory and have impacted her greatly. Again, we are all hardwired to connect with the Lord, and angels are a very biblical and current way for God to communicate to us.

## Clouds

Clouds are also surprisingly prominent in the Bible and often speak of God's presence and voice. God famously protected and guided Israel from the advancing armies of Egypt in a cloud.[33] We frequently see the cloud of God's presence descending on a tent, tabernacle, or temple where God's people and priests were either praying and worshiping or seeking Him for a specific direction.[34]

A few of my friends have experienced a cloud in their prayer and worship time. One of them had woken up in the middle of the night and felt like the Lord was calling her to pray and worship. She had spent a few hours just quietly worshiping the Lord when she noticed outside of her window a cloud. As she

---

32    Luke 2:10; Genesis 21; Acts 27

33    Exodus 13

34    Numbers 9, 12; Deuteronomy 5:22;I Kings 8:10; II Chronicles 5:13; Ezekiel 10:4; Mark 9:7; Revelations 14:14

continued with her devotions, she watched as the cloud outside began to move *inside* and fill her room. She was so freaked out that she ran downstairs to see if the gas on the stove had been left on, causing a fire and smoke. When she found that everything was in order, she went back to her room and realized that the cloud now filling her bedroom was the presence of God, and she rejoiced and reveled in His goodness.

This may sound very out-of-the-box for many which is honestly a good thing. If you can fit all that God does in your box, then you don't know Him that well. We must leave room for the wonder and mystery of God in how He chooses to speak to us. Again, if we see it in Scripture and in the life of Jesus on earth, we must be open to connecting with Him in every possible way.

## *Open Visions*

Earlier we discovered how visions from God-inspired pictures or movie-like reels are experienced in our seeing receptors. We also explored how visions are one of the ways God speaks to us with our internal sight. However, we find that God can also speak to us in an *open vision* which is our ability to physically see a spiritual reality. Let me give you an example from the life of the prophet Isaiah.

> *In the year that King Uzziah died, I saw the Lord, high and exalted, seated on a throne; Above him were seraphim, each with six wings; with two wings they covered their faces; with two they covered their feet, and with two they were flying.*
>
> Isaiah 6: 1-2

In this scripture, Isaiah had an open vision of what was happening in heaven in that exact moment. He *saw* with his natural eyes the Lord and the seraphim, covered with eyes, flying around Him. He was so aware of his unworthiness that he thought he would physically perish at just the sight of it. The gospel of Luke also recounts a story of how a *vision* of angels, proclaiming that Jesus was alive, appeared to some women. And it's not just those who are believers who can see in the spirit realm.

In the book of Acts, a Roman centurion named Cornelius had an open vision even though he did not know or believe in Jesus Christ. One afternoon, Cornelius *clearly saw* an angel of God, who came to him with a message; I love that the Bible tells us that Cornelius distinctly and plainly saw the angel in a vision. His mystical seeing receptor was fully engaged in that moment, and his response to what he saw set him and his family on a path to salvation. It's interesting to note again that Cornelius did not yet know Jesus when he had an encounter with the angel. This story again proves the truth that every person is hardwired to connect with God whether they are believers or not.

Blake Healy, an author, pastor, and speaker, has been involuntarily and consistently seeing physically into the spirit realm his entire life. Where some people like my sister have mystically seen the spirit realm maybe once or twice in their life, Blake sees angels and demons as clearly and as often as he sees the natural world around him. In fact, he records in his first book *The Veil*, that he didn't realize for years that most people couldn't see what he saw. He thought everyone was seeing the spirit and natural realm simultaneously just as he was. To get a glimpse into what it is like being a consistent mystical seer, I encourage you to read his books, *The Veil* and *Profound Good*. Both of these books are tremendous resources to help make us aware of what is available to us as children of God.

## *Trances*

Another way God speaks to us in our mystical sight receptor is through trances. The primary difference between a trance and an open vision is that a trance is a biblical word, describing an ecstatic state outside of one's normal mental or emotional position. This happens when what you are seeing in the mystical realm becomes more of a reality than your actual physical surroundings. Simply put, a vision or open vision is *watching a movie* while a trance is *participating in the movie*.

Larry Randolph describes trances as *"a displacement of the mind which gives a person a sense of detachment from their physical surroundings. While in this state, the mind and senses will often shut down, allowing the person to be overtaken by visual images."*[35] There also seems to be a biblical connection between prayer and a trance. The majority of people in the Bible that "fell into a trance" were praying. Perhaps prayer is the gateway into communing with God in this particular way.

One important distinction of biblical trances is that those who fell into a trance were hearing or seeing God himself. This is important to note because there are those within the New Age world who have illegitimately gone into trances to commune with spirit beings and demons. Again, the primary difference of a God-induced trance is that you are directly communicating with God, not other spirit beings.

---

35  *Spirit Talk,* by Larry Randolph, p.47

Peter the apostle while in a trance, received a message from God that radically shifted his perspective of Gentiles. In the book of Acts, we find him on the roof of a house, waiting for lunch to be prepared. As he was praying, the Bible records that he *fell into a trance.*[36] In this encounter, the Lord spoke to Peter through a vision about His heart and purpose to include the Gentiles in the message of salvation. It was this trance and vision that set Peter on the path to bring salvation to Cornelius and his family and set into motion the revelation that God has granted repentance for all who believe in Jesus' name.

God is speaking through the natural world around us and through the internal world within us, but He is also revealing and speaking through our physical sight into the spirit realm. He is speaking through His angels, open visions, trances, and other ways that we see by His Spirit. Do not discount what others are experiencing just because we have yet to experience what they have. It's also important to not get discouraged, make comparisons, or judgements about yourself if you haven't seen physically into the spirit realm. If anything, let the biblical knowledge of these things make you hungry to see God in every way because you've been hardwired to see him.

Here is a scriptural key to help increase spiritual sensitivity and the ability to see in the Spirit found in Proverbs.

> *Trust in the LORD with all of your heart*
> *and lean not on your own understanding.*
> *In all of your ways acknowledge Him*
> *and He will direct your path.*
>
> *Proverbs 3:5-6*

---

36  Acts 10:10

Practically, this is how it works: If I thought I saw a flash of light or a color, a lightness or darkness, a fog or cloudy-like substance, instead of dismissing it as nothing important, I would begin to acknowledge and thank the LORD. "Thank you, God, that I am seeing something. My eyes and my heart are open to You. Show me what You are doing." With that acknowledgment, often things will become clearer and stronger. The principle is that when you choose to not relegate these impressions only to the natural realm but rather acknowledge God in all of your perceptions, then you will gain greater clarity and direction.

Every type of seeing is meaningful, and all three realms are spiritual. What we see with our external, internal, and mystical seeing receptors can be a catalyst for encouragement, strengthening, and comfort in our lives and the lives of those around us. The goal is to develop our ability to see everything God has for us and to connect even deeper with the heart of the Father.

# CHAPTER 6

## EXTERNAL HEARING

*Hearing God through the world of natural sounds*

HAVE YOU EVER CAUGHT yourself hearing someone speaking but not really listening to what they are saying? This reminds me of the old Charlie Brown cartoons where Charlie Brown is at school and as his teacher is speaking, all he is hearing is "*Wah, wah, wah, wah, wah, wah.*" While the implication is that the teacher was speaking something intelligible, all Charlie was hearing were unintelligible words. It can sometimes feel similar to us as we learn to hear God speak.

God is speaking through the physical sounds in the world around us and because we have yet to recognize that it is *His* voice we are hearing, we don't process or receive His voice as intelligible. This is an example of hearing but not listening. Jesus challenged this particular issue many times in scripture when He would say, "*He who has ears to hear, let him hear.*"[37]

We know that God is *always* speaking. In fact, the phrase, *The Lord said,* appears over one thousand times in the scriptures!

---

37   Matthew 11:15

God is a communicating God; and just as we learned in the last section that seeing is passive but looking is active, in the same way hearing is passive but listening is active. The challenge for us is that we are not always listening. Jesus tells us in the gospel of John that those who belong to Him hear His voice. *"My sheep listen to My voice and I know them and they follow me."*[38] We are hardwired to literally hear God and to recognize His voice.

For example, if I see my children in a room full of people, I can call out any of their names and regardless of how noisy the room is, they will turn their attention to me. Why? Because they *know* the sound of my voice, they will *hear* my voice above every other voice and respond accordingly. In the same way, when we have attuned our hearts to know Him, we will instantly be able to recognize His voice above the clamor of other voices trying to get our attention. This is the power of hearing and recognizing God's voice to us.

A major key to discerning God's voice in the midst of a sea of voices can be found in Luke's gospel. Jesus taught the secrets of the kingdom of God in story form so that only those that were truly focusing their attention on learning could hear.

> He said, 'The knowledge of the secrets
> of the kingdom of God has been given
> to you, but to others I speak in parables,
> so that, through seeing, they may not see;
> through hearing, they may not understand.'
>
> *Luke 8:10*

---

38   John 10:27

60

Jesus is looking for the hungry listener. He is looking for those who will not just passively hear the sounds around them but will set their heart to *listen for God's voice* in the world around them. In the same way as we learned in earlier lessons to pay attention to what our eyes were drawn to as a source of spiritual information, we can also learn to listen for the word of the Lord in the world of sounds all around us. Let's explore a few different ways that God speaks through our external hearing receptors.

## Sounds of Creation

In the book of Genesis, we find an example of God speaking to Adam and Eve through their natural surroundings. The Bible records that they heard the *"sound of the Lord God walking in the garden in the cool of the day..."*[39] Another way to understand this scripture based on Hebrew definitions is that they heard the voice of God *in the wind of the day.* They heard a natural sound of wind and understood it to mean that God was speaking and was present in the garden with them. Adam and Eve had learned to recognize God's voice through the sounds of creation around them. He speaks to us through the stars and the skies,[40] and He is continually speaking through all the sounds of creation to those who have ears to hear.

## Sounds of People

Have you ever had a conversation with someone and as they were speaking, something they said — a phrase, a word —

---

39   Genesis 3:8

40   Psalms 19:1-2

hit your spirit like a bolt of lightning? There was something weightier behind their words, and it felt meaningful to you even if you didn't fully understand why. This has happened to me several times, but one that stands out took place several years ago.

I had been discussing with a friend of mine some options I was considering for my future. I could feel a personal upgrade coming to me but didn't quite know how it would manifest. This friend of mine told me, "*Bethany, if you take this position, it will set you back at least five years. You are called not primarily to the local ministry but internationally.*" We were just having a normal conversation, but when he said those words, it was like light bulbs turned on inside my spirit, and I *heard* God speaking to me through them.

> *So faith comes by hearing, and hearing by the word of Christ.*
>
> *Romans 10:17*

What you *hear* determines what you *believe*. What you believe determines your life choices and the action steps you will take. Interestingly, this passage indicates that faith is directly linked to what you choose to listen to, regardless of the voice. Additionally, this verse implies that if you're listening to the wrong voices, you will put your faith in the wrong things.

We saw this with the Israelites when twelve spies were sent out to investigate the Promised Land. Ten of the spies circulated a bad report of the land while two of them shared a good report of what the land held for those who believed God.[41] Which

---

41   Numbers 13

voice did the people of Israel listen to? Were they listening to God's promises that He had spoken through Joshua and Caleb, or were they putting their faith in the negative reports from the remaining ten spies?

> *And they (the ten spies) spread among the Israelites a bad report about the land they had explored...That night all the members of the community raised their voices and wept aloud. All the Israelites grumbled against Moses and Aaron, and the whole assembly said to them, "If only we had died in Egypt! Or in this wilderness! Why is the Lord bringing us to this land only to let us fall by the sword?"*[42]

Faith does come by hearing, and the Israelites chose to *hear* the negative reports. Your faith is directly proportional to the voice you are listening to. As believers, godly faith comes by listening to the voice of God. Unfortunately, that particular generation of Israelites forfeited their destiny, and Joshua and Caleb were the only ones who possessed the Promised Land because they had chosen to listen and believe God.

Our ability to hear and what we choose to listen to will impact our lives and our future for good or for bad. Right now, the narrative reports from every primary media source in my nation are unprecedented in the amount of fear, misinformation, and negative agenda it is pushing. And sadly, people are listening to this and putting their faith in what they hear. As a result, fear and division are rampant In America. I love this quote from a well-known speaker, *"Fear is faith in the wrong kingdom."*[43] What

---

42    Numbers 13:32, 14:1-3

43    Kris Vallotton

you hear affects what you believe which is why we must judge the voices we listen to.

We are hardwired to hear God speak through our external hearing, and it's our responsibility to recognize when He is talking to us. However, sometimes the people God speaks through can be personally offensive to us. Let's look at another type of external hearing through people in this unique biblical example.

Caiaphas was high-priest at the time of Jesus and was a strategic figure in plotting Jesus' crucifixion.[44] The Pharisees were frantic that they would lose their religious status and their nation as so many Jews were converting and believing in Jesus. In the midst of this council, Caiaphas stands up and declares:

> 'You know nothing at all! You do not realize that it is better for you that one man die for the people than that the whole nation perish.' He did not say this on his own, but as high priest that year he prophesied that Jesus would die for the Jewish nation.
>
> John 11:49-51

What's interesting here is that Scripture records that Caiaphas was prophesying and yet Caiaphas was not trying to prophesy. He literally proclaimed Jesus' purpose for coming though neither he nor those around him comprehended it. He thought he was just making a persuasive statement to get the outcome he wanted–Jesus' death. God speaks even through common statements, and for those who have an 'ear to hear' they will recognize the Lord's voice through whichever vessel

---

44   John 18

He chooses to speak through, even if that vessel is offensive to you. Maturity in hearing increases when you can hear God speaking to you regardless of the source.

For example, did you know that one of the primary people in the Old Testament who foretold the connection of the star with the Messiah's birth was Balaam, who was considered a false prophet?[45] The Magi knew how to locate the Messiah because of Balaam's prophecy, and they did not let their personal judgment of his poor character deter them from recognizing God's voice through his words. God doesn't throw the baby out with the bath water, and we shouldn't either just because we don't like who's drawing the water. God is speaking through the people around us. Our job is to recognize when it's His voice resonating through our normal, everyday conversations.

Almost two decades ago, I was part of a leadership team of a small, start-up young-adult church in the mountains. It was the "cool snowboard" church where many of the transient young adults would attend during their time as ski and snowboard instructors on the local mountain. During a prayer meeting with our core leadership group, I remember I was struggling with a decision I had made about something. In my mind, I was literally thinking the thoughts, *Lord, I think I made a mistake in this matter,* when a spiritual father who was praying for all of us suddenly leaned over and quietly said *"The Lord says you did not make a mistake."* I was undone. It was like I was having this private conversation with the Lord in my head, and He literally answered my question a few seconds later through another person. This spiritual father had no knowledge of my inner-dialogue with the Lord nor had he any "natural" reason to say that

---

45    See Numbers 24:17-19

to me. He was being the voice of God and releasing the heart of the Father to me at that moment.

God speaks through people, and sometimes he doesn't use words. Once as part of a ministry team in Australia, we were asked to speak encouraging words and life over people at a special leader's gathering. One of the young ladies on our team called up an Aboriginal woman. Our team member told this woman that although she didn't have any English words, God was giving her *various sounds* to speak over her. So, she proceeded to speak-sing over this Aboriginal woman in unintelligible sounds, clicks, and hums. To be honest, the rest of our team was looking around, wondering who was going to clean up this potential mess because in the natural world, it made no sense.

When our team member finished speaking these sounds, the Aboriginal leader was in tears. She shared that what was spoken over her was an Aboriginal bush call that she hadn't heard since she was a child. The Lord was speaking to this woman through a physical sound that was particularly meaningful to her even though it sounded like nonsense to the rest of us. God speaks your language. He knows how to communicate to you in meaningful ways that perhaps only you can truly understand.

Another way we can hear God speak externally through people often happens in church. Have you ever been in a church service where you felt completely singled out by the preacher because it seemed like they were speaking directly to you? I have pastor friends who told me once that one of their church members would come up to them extremely upset because they thought the messages the pastors were preaching were specifically created and aimed towards him. Of course, my pastor friends had no idea what was going on personally with this church member. They had been just speaking what God had told them to say, and apparently, it was hitting its mark.

Pay attention next time God speaks to you through people. You will know it is Him by how it lands in and on you. Your spirit will feel a resonation or "bear witness" with the words being spoken.[46] It's almost as if the words or sounds spoken become larger than life to you, and it hits your spirit in a way that makes something come alive in you. More often than not, we have all experienced God's voice in this way but perhaps have quickly dismissed it as "it's just me." I want to encourage you that the next time you encounter His voice in this way, just respond to His voice in faith. He is speaking through what you hear in the people around you.

## *Movies, songs, audiobooks and podcasts*

Another way that the Lord loves to speak to us in the realm of external hearing is through movies, songs, and any other creative medium that involves listening like audiobooks and podcasts.

Did you know that creativity is not a gift or a mood but rather a part of our God-given nature as *creators.*[47] We were created to create because we are made in the image of the Creator. Therefore, anything created or creative can speak of His nature.[48] When we are watching movies or listening to music, God can speak through those mediums because the authors of those movies are functioning in their God-given nature as creators.

---

46    Romans 8:16

47    Dan McCollam ref.

48    Romans 1:20

This doesn't mean that everything we hear is God-inspired, but it does mean that those who have "ears to hear" will recognize God speaking when He is highlighting something.

For example, how many of you have been impacted by some of the dialogue in blockbuster movies like *Narnia* or *Lord of the Rings?* Each of these parabolic stories were written by Christians even though the stories aren't strictly Christian. Now, what about other movies and songs that are not written by Christians? Can we hear God speak through them? Yes, if we have ears to hear what the Lord is choosing to speak to us in that moment. Again, it is our responsibility to recognize His voice and not judge the messenger it's coming through.

One of my favorite superhero movies is *Black Panther.* I remember when I first saw it in the movie theater. I loved the storyline, the setting in Africa, the colorful costumes, the music– everything. But there was one particular moment in the movie that really impacted me when the hero was fighting in a battle, and it looked like for a moment he was about to lose his kingship to his opponent. Just as our hero was about to go down, his eyes focused on his mother, the queen, whose voice came forth and pierced not just the theater but my spirit. She shouted, *"Show him who you are!"* It was like she was speaking directly to me and not the character in the movie. At that moment, I heard God speak through that powerful phrase, through the script of a non-Christian movie, and I suddenly saw how I needed to live and act in the fullness of who God says I am. It was time for me to "show up" and be me.

What about God speaking through songs? There have been many strategic moments in my life where I needed to hear God's specific thoughts about something with which I was dealing, and I have asked Him to speak to me through a song. One particular time, I remember I had been really struggling with my identity. I needed to know how He felt about me and if I had "messed up" too many times for Him to use me. So, I prayed and selected shuffle on my iPhone music. Suddenly a song came on that spoke radically to my identity; it was like God Himself was singing to me through the music. I had actually never heard of that song before and had no idea how it had even gotten on my playlist. To this day, I still don't know the name of that song or could even find it again. Yet, God in His goodness chose to speak to me through this song that broke off the lies that I was believing and set me on a path of hope once again.

God speaks through our external hearing receptors. He is speaking through the sounds we physically hear around us whether they are in creation, people, or even the media. Learn to actively listen when something you hear ignites your spirit in a fresh or meaningful way as the Lord is trying to get your attention. He is not silent. Learn to listen. Lean in to His voice and you will hear Him in the world of sounds around you.

# CHAPTER 7

## INTERNAL HEARING

*Hearing God through the Internal Realm*

D ID YOU KNOW YOU CAN "hear" your thoughts? Even now as
you are reading these words, you are not just processing
them through your mind, but you are internally hearing yourself read them. You're not just thinking your thoughts; you are
hearing your thoughts. Dr. Kulreet Chudhary, a neuroscien-
tist and pioneer in the field of Integrative Medicine,[49] says this
about hearing our thoughts. *"Sound includes the entire world of
vibrations, including our thoughts. Our thoughts are audible to us,
and they can directly and indirectly impact our cellular health."*[50]

Our inner voice or internal dialogue is experienced as thoughts
in our head, and studies have shown that the inner voice speaks
up to ten times faster than the average human speaking voice.[51]

---

49  https://drkulreetchaudhary.com/biography/

50  Cleaning Up the Mental Mess with Dr. Caroline Leaf

51  https://www.theatlantic.com/science/archive/2016/11/figuring-out-how-
and-why-we-talk-to-ourselves/508487/

This means that you are hearing a massive amount of information from your inner voice at any given moment. I tend to process my thoughts externally, and I am sure many are thankful that external processors can't process verbally as quickly as their inner dialogue.

This inner dialogue constantly interjects thoughts into our minds that affect a person's identity, personality, mood, and destiny. Your thoughts are vital to your self-talk because what you think becomes the voice you "listen" to. And what you listen to shapes your belief system, and which ultimately will express itself through your actions. The voice you listen to is the voice you will act on. Perhaps, this is why the philosopher Rene Descartes said these famous words: *I think, therefore I am.*

There is a war over your thought life and the enemy works overtime to get you to listen to his lies, but fortunately, he's not the only voice speaking to us. God is speaking, too.

When we receive Christ as our Savior a new voice moves in. Although God's voice has always been speaking to you–before you were born again–the moment you asked Jesus into your life, He began residing *inside* of you. The Holy Spirit begins to speak to your heart and spirit. He begins to reveal the very thoughts of God.

*Now God has revealed these things to us by His Spirit*
*Since the Spirit searches everything, even the depths of God.*
*For who knows a person's thoughts except his spirit within him?*
*In the same way, no one knows the thoughts of God*
*except the Spirit of God.*
*Now we have not received the spirit of the world,*
*But the Spirit who comes from God,*
*So that we may understand what has*

*Been freely given to us by God…*
*We have the mind of Christ.*

*1 Corinthians 2:10-12,16*

God reveals His thoughts *to* us by His Spirit *within* us. Because the Spirit knows and searches everything, we can hear God's thoughts in our heart and mind. If you can hear your inner voice or dialogue, then you can hear God's voice speaking to you internally. Once you begin to recognize God's voice in your heart, it can become like a fire or a fountain of revelation.

Hearing God internally was the first way I started practicing hearing God speak to me. I was deeply impacted by Mark Virkler's book, *Dialogue with God,* that clarified for me how God speaks to us through our inner voice and how to know it is His voice and not my own or the enemy's.

One of the practical instructions I learned to help grow in this arena was to get a journal and begin writing to the Lord. I would write my thoughts and heart to the Lord, and then I would ask Him a question. After I asked the Lord a question, I would listen to the thoughts/voice that would come to me and start journaling what I had heard. I wouldn't question or judge what I was hearing yet. I just wrote and let it flow out of me and continued journaling that exchange back and forth between my thoughts and His.

It was this regular practice that caused me to grow confident in His voice speaking to me internally. Obviously, it was important to go back through what I had written down and judge according to the protocols set forth later on in this book, but this practice of journaling to hear Him internally was invaluable to my process of recognizing His voice.

Let's look at some ways that God speaks to us through our internal hearing receptors. As you read through these descriptions, pay attention to any memories the Lord is highlighting to you. He could be revealing how you have already been hearing Him speak to your internal realm, and He wants to affirm that. If you haven't experienced any of these ways God speaks yet, let this be an exciting new adventure to practice and grow in.

## *Still, Small Voice*

The prophet Elijah was having a really bad day, and he needed to hear from God. In the first book of Kings, Elijah had just experienced one of the greatest victories of his life where fire had fallen from heaven and consumed his soggy sacrifice. The double-minded crowd had seen in that moment that definitively *"the LORD, He IS God."* After this display of God's power, the Israelite mob drew together as one to remove the false prophets from the land which was a victory for the nation of Israel and the Lord. Meanwhile, as a result of the destruction of the false prophets of Baal, Israel's evil queen Jezebel grew even more determined in her heart to hunt down and murder Elijah.

As Elijah escapes with his life, he walks for forty days and nights to meet God on Mount Horeb. We can imagine that the prophet was emotionally and physically exhausted after all of these events. His dialogue leads us to believe that he was struggling with depression and fear, and it was from this dark place that he cried out to God. God instructed him to go on the mountain of the Lord and to wait for God to speak. We catch up with this narrative in the nineteenth chapter.

> *And behold, the Lord passed by, and a great and strong*
> *wind tore into the mountains and broke the rocks in pieces be-*
> *fore the Lord, but the Lord was not in the wind; and after the*

*wind an earthquake, but the Lord was not in the earthquake; and after the earthquake a fire, but the Lord was not in the fire; and after the fire a still small voice. So it was, when Elijah heard it, that he wrapped his face in his mantle and went out and stood in the entrance of the cave. Suddenly a voice came to him, and said, 'What are you doing here, Elijah?'*

*I Kings 19:11-13*

It's interesting to note that God had previously shown up in Israel's history in the wind, earthquakes, and fire, so it was not unreasonable for Him to reveal Himself that way again.[52] Yet, Elijah recognized that God was not speaking through those forms this time. God doesn't always speak in the same ways that He has in the past. He is often doing a new thing, and it is our communion with Him that allows us to recognize when and how He is speaking in the new thing. This is why it is so important to activate *all* our receptors to hear what God is saying to us.

Many seeking God's voice want Him to speak loud and demonstratively like the rushing wind, the shaking earthquake, and the blazing fire. *Make it loud and clear so I can't miss it!* And, although God *can* speak in that way, He is often found in the still small voice. This voice is often less perceived with the ears and more heard with the heart. God is looking for those who would lean in to His whisper.

Going back to Elijah's story, we really see the kindness of the Lord shown to Elijah in how He chose to speak with the despondent prophet. Elijah was feeling discouraged and dejected, and the Lord didn't speak to him in a loud, spectacular, "blow you out of the water" way like He often did with Moses. No, he knew

---

52  Exodus 3:3; Ex. 19:18; Jonah 1:4

where Elijah was personally and in His kindness, He came in a gentle voice. Have you ever had a conversation with someone who is whispering or speaking softly? What usually happens in that exchange? You have to get closer to them so you can hear them more clearly. In the same way the Lord will speak in His kind, gentle, and almost whisper-like voice, which compels me to draw closer to Him to hear what He is saying.

Years ago, I was at a church as part of a ministry team, and I was having a conversation with a young woman when suddenly I heard an internal quiet voice say, *She is pregnant*. As she was speaking, I scanned her up and down and concluded that she, in fact, did *not* look pregnant. I didn't say anything, but as she continued talking, I kept hearing a still, small voice tell me she was pregnant. Now, I don't know about you, but it's not usually considered encouraging for women to be asked if they are pregnant when they are not, and particularly if they don't look pregnant. Though I didn't want to insult her, I couldn't shake the voice, so I decided to step out in faith. I began by asking her if she and her husband were wanting to get pregnant soon, and then I just blurted out, *"In fact, are you pregnant? Because I keep hearing you are pregnant!"*

After I said that, she quietly confided to me that, in fact, she was pregnant but they hadn't told anyone yet as her pregnancy was still early. She continued to disclose that due to much bleeding, she had just been in the emergency room the day before. They were concerned that they had lost their first baby but wouldn't know the results for at least a week. In that moment, faith rose up within me, and I told her boldly, *"God told me you ARE pregnant, not WERE pregnant, so I believe that you are still carrying that baby!"* I then prayed over her, her body, and the baby.

Two weeks later, I received a text from her saying that they had received the results, and she was still pregnant! She said it had been the hardest week for her and her husband, not knowing if she was carrying this child or not, but the word from the Lord that she was still pregnant kept them going in faith. Months later, she sent me a picture of her beautiful, healthy, baby girl who is their joy and delight.

A friend of mine was washing dishes one day when she heard the Lord speak to her in this internal way and asked her to stop what she was doing and to go buy groceries for a particular person. She didn't even know what groceries to buy or if the person was in need or not. However, because she had grown accustomed to hearing the Lord in this manner, she knew it was Him and proceeded to obey.

She went to the grocery store and bought what she felt was needed and then drove to this person's house to drop them off. She laid the groceries on the front door step, rang the doorbell, and left before the person opened the door. A few hours later, my friend called this person to see how they were doing and if they had received the groceries. The woman answered the phone sobbing and began to relay to my friend how she had had no money, and there was no more food left in the house. She expressed how thankful and blessed she was by the groceries. God was able to provide for this person's need through my friend because she had learned to recognize and respond to His voice speaking to her internally.

Another friend of mine recently recovered from the worst viral cold she had ever had. During the first week or so, she was getting progressively worse to the point that she was having difficulty breathing. Finally, she woke up one night and prayed to the Lord, *God, I need your help. If something doesn't change in my body, I'm going to need to go to the hospital tomorrow!* To which she immediately heard the Lord speak internally to her, *You don't need to go to the hospital. You'll be fine. You just need to drink some water.* After she heard Him speak to her, she realized that she had drank very little water in the last few days and was probably dehydrated on top of all her other symptoms. She started drinking water and was very intentional about it throughout the next few days, and immediately she saw a shift in her health recovery.

God speaks to us in the still, small voice that often expresses itself as unsolicited thoughts in our mind and heart. What is God speaking to you?

## *Songs of the heart*

Have you ever woken up in the morning with a song in your heart or hummed a tune during the day that was unrelated to any music you had recently been listening to? Solomon's book of song reveals that while we are sleeping, our hearts are awake listening for the voice of the One who loves us.[53] Could it be that the song you wake up with is the song the LORD was singing over you in the night? Did you know that this is one of the ways that God speaks to us in our internal hearing receptors? Zephaniah 3:17 tells us that:

> *The Lord your God in your midst,*
> *The Mighty One, will save;*
> *He will rejoice over you with gladness,*
> *He will quiet you with His love,*
> *He will rejoice over you with singing.*

---

53   Song of Solomon 5:2

God rejoices over you with singing. He is singing songs over your life right now, and those who have ears to hear will catch His melodies. God sings over us because He's looking for our agreement. When we sing what He is singing, we are agreeing with His voice over our life which then can accelerate His purposes.

I remember for at least two years, I would be particularly drawn to songs about seasons shifting, both worship and marketplace songs. I would wake up hearing these melodies in my heart and be singing them throughout the day. Sometimes they were songs I knew, and other times they were these spontaneous melodies. At the time, I did not realize that it was the Lord singing over me. It wasn't until much later that I looked back and saw how He had sung me into my new season. By singing over me, He was preparing my heart for the season shift that was coming, and every time I would sing those songs, I was agreeing with His will and adding my *amen* to His *yes* over my life. Pay attention to the songs that you *listen* to in your heart. Dialogue with the Holy Spirit about them. He could very well be singing you into your next season.

## Hearing in Visions and Dreams

We usually think of dreams and visions as a visual message only, but often we can hear God speak as well through these types of encounters. In the Old Testament, God identified dreams and visions as a primary way that He would speak to His prophets. Let's look at what He said in the book of Numbers:

> *Hear now my words:*
> *If there is a prophet among you,*

> *I, the LORD, shall make myself*
> *known to him in a vision,*
> *I shall speak with him in a dream.*
>
> *Numbers 12:6*

God speaking to us through dreams and visions is not meant to be exclusive or exceptional. We see in the Bible that God took the initiative to speak to prophets through visions and dreams, but it wasn't just the particularly gifted or important people who heard Him speak in dreams. Kings, queens, children, men, women, slaves, prisoners, and prophets are all recorded as those who heard God speaking to them this way through their internal hearing receptors. We also know that in the New Testament, dreams and visions were part of the outpouring of the Spirit on *all* flesh. Everyone can now hear God's voice speak in and through visions and dreams.[54]

Sometimes we hear God speaking to us in this realm, and it can take place during the in-between state of sleeping and waking. I remember one time as I was just waking up and coming to a conscious state, I heard a voice speaking to me, *"Write the vision down and make it plain so the runners can run."* It was so loud in my spirit that it almost felt like a shout. I recognized those words from the book of Habakkuk,[55] leading me on a journey with the Lord about its meaning in my life.

Though similar, *hearing* God speak in dreams and visions is different than *seeing* God speak in dreams and visions. With visions and dreams, we can recognize God speaking in our internal sight by the visual pictures that He brings to

---

54    Acts 2:17

55    Habakkuk 2:2

mind. In hearing God through visions and dreams, we are identifying His voice through what we *hear internally* and not so much the pictures or visual images. He is speaking through visions and dreams in both receptors, but the way we recognize His voice is distinctive. One way we *see* and the other we *hear*. Daniel gives us a great example; although he was watching a vision, it was what he heard– not saw–that was the message.

> *While I, Daniel, was watching the vision and trying to understand it, there before me stood one who looked like a man. And I heard a man's voice from the Ulai calling, 'Gabriel, tell this man the meaning of the vision.'*
>
> Daniel 8:15-16

Daniel needed to hear before he could understand what he saw. This is not to say that we don't often both see and hear simultaneously. In fact, there is a strong biblical partnership between all of the receptors that we call *spiritual synesthesia* which we will touch on briefly later in this book.

## *Bring to Remembrance*

Did you know that one of the ways God speaks to you is to remind you of what He has already said? The apostle John tells us that:

> *...the Helper, the Holy Spirit, whom the Father will send in my name, he will teach you all things and bring to your remembrance all that I have said to you...*
>
> John 14:26

The Greek definition of the word *remembrance* means *to remind quietly, i.e., suggest to the (middle voice, one's own) memory.* God speaks to us by causing us to remember things He has said or done. There are things that the Lord is currently speaking to you by causing you to remember what He has formerly said to you. This in essence, is the power of testimony.

The book of Revelation tells us the testimony of Jesus is the spirit of prophecy[56] which means that when Jesus has done something wonderful in the past for someone else, that testimony is speaking to His ability and desire to do the same for you. If Jesus healed and delivered your neighbor, He can do the same for you. Jesus provided for your needs in the past, and He is able to do it again. Why? Because He is the same yesterday, today and forever; and what He did yesterday, He will surely do tomorrow. Perhaps not in the same way as he did it yesterday, but He will still do it because that is who He is. He *is* Healer. He *is* Provider. And our ability to *call to remembrance* testimonies or words that He spoke in our past experiences can pull those breakthroughs into our today. The weeping prophet Jeremiah understood the power of remembrance.

> *This I recall to my mind, therefore I have hope. Through the Lord's mercies we are not consumed, because His compassions fail not. They are new every morning; great is Your faithfulness.*
>
> *Jeremiah 3:21-23*

It was Jeremiah's ability to *call to mind* or remember who the Lord is and what He has said that propelled him into an atti-

---

56   Revelations 19:10

tude of hope and expectancy for his current situation. Reminding ourselves to think the way God does about situations–even from our past–is a way God communicates to us.

Listen to this powerful story about how the Lord spoke to my friend Tracy by calling to her remembrance a truth that had had a profound impact on her life.

*I wasn't raised with any religion or belief system. I didn't even hear the name of Jesus until I was twenty-two. I had heard of God but never Jesus. As I have gotten older and have grown in my faith and walk with Jesus, I have been curious about my life as a child with God since the scripture says "I knew you before you were formed". He knew me, but I didn't know him? Or did I?*

*I began to ask God to show me our encounters together when I was growing up, and to my surprise, there were so many of them! I just didn't recognize them. He reminded me of that time when I was ten years old when I was walking through my neighborhood and felt compelled to just walk into a church in the middle of the day during the week. That was Him. He told me He led me there. He also awakened the memory of the annual Ten Commandments movie that would come on TV at Easter. As a child, I was glued to that movie and was so fascinated and moved emotionally by it even though I couldn't understand why. That was Him.*

*I realize now that there were many encounters throughout my life as a child that I had with a God I didn't know. It was comforting to me to realize He was always with me even when I didn't know it was Him at the time. Perhaps God was reintroducing himself to me and now I have a whole new lens of Him.*

*Perhaps God was reintroducing Himself to me...*

What a powerful statement. Here is a woman in her mid-years of life, who wanted to know where God was as a child before she had known Him. And it was through *remembrance* that He spoke to her and revealed how He had been reaching out to her throughout her life. This encounter shifted how she viewed God and even her past childhood because she was now viewing it through the lens of God's voice and presence in her life.

Allow God to call to mind His voice in your life. It could be through scriptures, specific things He has promised you, or even as in Tracy's story, memories now seen through the love lens of a loving Father, who was drawing you even before you knew it was Him. God speaks to us today by calling or re-calling to mind things we may have forgotten, but when He reintroduces it to us in our present, it can be the beginning of a fresh and new conversation that will deepen our connection with Him.

God is speaking through the natural realm around you, but He is also speaking to your internal realm through your thoughts and inner voice. He is singing over you with songs to catch your attention and agreement for His will in your life. He is speaking and bringing direction to you through His voice in your dreams and visions, and He is bringing to your remembrance His presence in your life—both past and present, realized and unrealized. You are hardwired to hear him internally.

# CHAPTER 8

## MYSTICAL HEARING

*Hearing God speak audibly in the Spirit Realm*

I N THE LAST TWO CHAPTERS, we have discovered that we can hear God speaking through the sounds of the natural realm around us and also through the still, small voice in the internal realm within us. In this chapter, let's explore how we are hard-wired to hear Him in the heavenly or spirit realm. Simply defined, this is *hearing with our physical ears the audible sounds and voices of the heavenly realm.* How awesome is it that God communicates to His sons and daughters in this way? There are many recorded instances in scripture where the audible voice of God or His angels spoke to people, and they heard Him. It is also important to note that there is no biblical account that proves that God ever stopped speaking audibly; therefore, we can and should expect that He still speaks audibly today.

Many of those who heard the audible voice of the Lord throughout the scriptures describe it as *the sound of many waters,*[57]

---

57    Revelations 14:2

*thunder[58]* and *harpists playing on their harp.*[59]There are multiple accounts throughout scripture when prophets, priests, kings, and leaders heard the audible voice of God. Once again, the key to growing in any receptor is learning to recognize and respond to the ways He is currently speaking. For example, before he was ever a prophet, the young boy Samuel heard the Lord audibly call his name three times. Thinking that it was the priest Eli calling his name, each time the child ran to Eli saying *"Here I am!"* Only to be told by Eli to go back to bed. God was speaking to Samuel literally—not through natural, earthly sounds or through an internal voice. It was God's voice speaking just like we would talk and physically hear one another.[60]

God also spoke audibly to Moses just as a man speaks to his friend, face-to-face.[61] Elijah the prophet heard God speak audibly to him when he was on Mt. Horeb. Scriptures record that, *"...suddenly a voice came to Him."*[62] The Hebrew word for voice is *qowl* which means *voice, sound, noise,* so we can conclude he encountered the Lord audibly in this mystical way of hearing. When Jesus was being baptized by John the Baptist in the Jordan river, the heavens opened and the voice of the Father declared audibly, *"This is My Son, in whom I am well-pleased."*[63]

However, one of the strangest passages in scripture related to the audible voice of God is found in the book of John. I believe this passage gives us some clues on how we can identify

58    Revelations 14:2, Psalms 29:3-4

59    Psalms 33:2

60    I Samuel 3

61    Exodus 33:11

62    I Kings 19:13

63    Matthew 3:17

and respond to the audible voice of God. Let's pick up the account in chapter twelve where Jesus is praying to the Father in front of a crowd.

> *Father, glorify your name!'*
> *Then a voice came from heaven,*
> *I have glorified it, and will glorify it again.'*
> *The crowd that was there and heard it said it had thundered;*
> *Others said an angel had spoken to him.*
> *Jesus answered, 'This voice has come for your sake, not mine....'*
> *John 12:28-29*

Notice, there were three responses to the audible voice of God. First, they all heard the same sound but interpreted it differently. Next, some thought it had thundered while others recognized it as being spiritual but did not attribute it directly to God's voice. And, finally, there were those who knew it was the voice of God. Let's explore each of these groups of people for a greater understanding in hearing God's audible voice for us today.

## 1. Natural realm:

*Some said it had thundered*. While we have already discussed that God does speak through the external created realm, this circumstance was different. There were those who literally heard the audible voice of God but attributed it to the natural realm. How often do we do this? As humans, we like things to be explainable, to fit into our nice little box of limited understanding. Unfortunately, if something doesn't fit, we can easily dismiss God's voice and explain it away with our natural minds.

This brings up an important question. Why were there so many different responses to the same voice? What factor determined what people heard when the audible voice of God spoke? The answer is most likely that their expectation was formed from their belief system. Many believe God no longer speaks today and certainly not audibly. When God speaks to this group, they will always attribute it to natural causes. They will assume, *Oh, that's just me. That's my imagination.* They hear the voice of God but reason it away because of their unbelief.

However, attributing the voice of God to a natural source can also come simply from the ignorance of not knowing God. Let's look at the boy Samuel again. Samuel grew up in a time when the word of the LORD was rare, and the Bible records there were not many visions.[64] God spoke to the young boy audibly and called his name, but because Samuel had never heard God's voice before, he thought it was the voice of the priest Eli. The priest had to help the young boy recognize and respond to the voice of God. And the beautiful thing is that once Samuel learned to recognize God's voice, scripture records he never let one of God's words fall to the ground—meaning he treasured God's voice and obeyed everything he heard. [65]

## 2. Spirit realm:

*Some said it was an angel.* This group acknowledged that something spiritual and unexplainable had happened but did not attribute it directly to God. We also have this camp of people today who believe that something spiritual is happening,

64   I Samuel 3:1

65   I Samuel 3:19

but they do not believe it is God. Many church people in our generation would say it is the devil while those who identify themselves as New Age people might be quick to say the voice was an angel, a spirit guide, or a spirit being.

This brings up an important point: We must rightly discern the source of these spiritual voices we are audibly hearing. Not every voice we hear audibly is God's or one of His angel's voices. Unfortunately, there are many people in this world who hear demonic voices telling them to do horrific things to themselves and others. Many of these people may have abused themselves with drugs, be involved in the occult, or may even have a brain disorder.

I have a very close friend who was struggling with a mental disorder and would hear voices telling him he should just take his own life and that his family would be better off without him. He was a believer, and he loved Jesus; and the only thing that kept him from listening to those voices was knowing that God would not be honored or pleased with him taking his life. This is where community and testing the word is vital in processing what you believe you are hearing from God. When we are able to bring those we respect and those who carry wisdom into our process, we will be able to discern and rightly divide those voices that are masquerading as an *angel of light* from the true voice of the Lord.[66] This is also why we must know the character and nature of God through His Word and His Son. Remember, *anything* that is contrary or outside of the nature and character of Jesus Christ is to be questioned and judged.

While it is important to discern God's voice from the demonic, we must not let the pendulum swing to the opposite

---

66    I Corinthians 14:29

extreme like some did in Jesus' time. While there are those who believe that spiritual forces are at work in the world, they don't expect God Himself to speak. These people are often so afraid of being deceived that even when God does speak, they don't trust that it is truly from Him.

Even today, there are self-appointed "watchdog" groups that are looking for anyone who might be considered a false prophet, false teacher, or under demonic deception. In Jesus' time, this is the same group that said he was of the devil. They attributed all of the miracles of Jesus to demons and his teaching to demon possession.[67] Beware of those who always want to point the finger and criticize. Fear of being deceived will never produce godly results because perfect love casts out fear. Fear of deception closes the door to love's call. I am certainly not saying we should be ignorant or gullible, but we also cannot live with fear as our operating system, or we will miss the voice of God.

## 3. God's voice:

When the Father responded to Jesus' prayer, John knew it was the audible voice of God speaking. Remember, Jesus said, *"My sheep know my voice."* John had been with Jesus and was able to recognize and identify the voice of the Father speaking audibly. This is the group we want to be a part of, acknowledging and celebrating that God speaks in many ways today–even audibly.

So, which camp would you be in? Those that did not recognize that the sound they heard was God audibly speaking

---

67    Luke 11:15-19

or those that are believing and expecting that God is speaking to His sons and daughters today? With so many accounts of the audible voice of God in both the Old and New Testament, shouldn't we be more expectant to actually hear God speak to us through our mystical hearing receptors? Your faith position will affect your hearing perspective. Obviously, God Himself chooses how He speaks to you whether externally, internally, or mystically. However, the point is God *is* speaking. Are you hearing? Now, let's look at some practical ways we can recognize God speaking to us through the mystical hearing realm.

## *Audible voice of God*

We've already talked a lot about how God has spoken audibly to people throughout the Bible, but what about today? Does He still speak audibly to people today? Let's be encouraged by this testimony from a friend of mine where the Lord spoke to her audibly about her future before she was even saved.

> *When I was in my early twenties, I was on the verge of suicide and in the darkest place in my life after years of drugs, alcohol and abusive relationships. My life was reduced to one box of belongings. At the time, I was renting a room from a known drug dealer, so I wouldn't be on the streets. One night sitting on the couch, two guys walked in to buy some marijuana. I glanced up as they walked into the door, and immediately I heard an audible voice speak loudly. This voice said, 'That is your husband.' I didn't know God and had never heard of Jesus, so I thought I was crazy until I found out that the man who was highlighted to me had heard the same voice except, he had heard, 'That is your wife.'*

*I came to know God through His audible voice speaking to me. We don't have to be believers before He speaks to us! When He speaks, He creates. One year later we were married, and three years later I said yes to Jesus. Often when I tell this story, it challenges a religious mindset that says God doesn't speak to non-believers or that He doesn't speak audibly, but He did to me that day and gave me thirty-one years of marriage and three beautiful children when I never even expected to live to see twenty-four years.*

What a powerful testimony of God audibly speaking to someone about her future and then leading her to Him. This is the reason He speaks, to lead us into a deeper revelation and relationship with Himself.

## *Heavenly sounds*

There are also times when God speaks or reveals Himself through sounds that are seemingly natural or earthly but have a heavenly root. Heaven and earth often have similar patterns, so it makes sense that they might have similar sounds.[68] The primary difference here between hearing externally and mystically is that the seemingly earthly sound does not have its source in a natural occurrence. Though it sounds like a natural thing, it's actually coming from the spirit realm. A simple example of this can be found in the book of Acts when a group of people were in one place, in one accord, and then the *wind* came.

---

68    Hebrews 8:5

*And suddenly there came a sound from heaven, as of a rushing mighty wind, and it filled the whole house where they were sitting.*

*Acts 2:2*

Notice it was the sound of a *rushing mighty wind* from heaven, but it was not actually an earthly, natural wind. The recognizable sound of wind was connected to a heavenly reality. It was a Holy Ghost hurricane.

In the Old Testament, when Samaria was under siege by the king of Aram, the siege lasted so long that there was a terrible and great famine in the city. In fact, if something didn't drastically change soon, everyone was on their last meal. Four lepers sitting at the entrance of the city gate decided that their chances of survival would be best if they were to go and surrender to the Aramean army. They figured they were certainly going to die if they stayed where they were in Samaria, so they took a risk by heading to the enemy camp, looking for mercy. What they found was even better as they approached the camp of the Arameans. The entire camp was empty with every tent completely abandoned. What had happened? What could have caused this massive army with only the clothes on their backs to leave in such haste? God happened with a sound.

*...for the Lord had caused the Arameans to hear the sound of chariots and horses and a great army, so that they said to one another, 'Look, the king of Israel has hired the Hittite and Egyptian armies to attack us!' So they got up and fled in the dusk...*

*II Kings 7:6-7a*

Heaven created the sound of marching armies and horses which caused such fear in the Aramean armies, they fled for their lives. It was an earthly sound but from a heavenly source. Interestingly, the entire army heard the sound, not just the select few, which proves again the point that we are all hardwired to hear Him.

A friend of mine had an encounter years ago with a heavenly sound. He was playing guitar for a worship team during a revival meeting, and there came a point in time that the worship leader began to spontaneously sing the words *"Send the fire"* over and over. As the leader sang this, there suddenly was a physical sound of a wind blowing through the place. At first, only a few people on the worship team could hear it, and they began to ask each of the musicians if it was them making the sound on their instruments, but no one was. The leader continued to sing about the wind and the fire of God, and each time he sang those words, it was as if Heaven was responding with its own agreement by sending the sound of wind. The longer he did this, the more people would catch on to the sound of heaven and rejoice in His presence. This mystical sound encounter went on for at least half an hour and was recorded on video. Heaven was responding to the worship and cry of the people with the sound of a heavenly wind.

## *Angels and worship*

One of the more common testimonies I've heard from people in mystical hearing is in the context of worship. Recently, one of our primary worship leaders related how she had heard angels singing for the very first time during the worship set she was leading. In fact, she was trying so intently to hear what they

94

were singing that she almost got distracted from leading worship! My friend shared this experience of audibly hearing God's voice and the heavenly realm.

> *Though I have only had a few instances of hearing the audible voice of God, they were powerful and shaped my life significantly. One of the things that I have noticed about the audible voice is that even when God is speaking out loud, not everyone hears it. The first time I heard the audible voice of God, He was singing over me. I was in a crowded room, but only I heard it. I could definitely hear it with my ears and I remember being in awe of the experience but also surprised others could not hear it.*
>
> *In other instances, during worship the heavenly realm would open up and I would hear angels singing or playing instruments. One time while this was happening, the pastor's son noticed a look of awe on my face. He asked me what was going on, and I reached out to grab his arm and pull him closer. When I touched him, his ears opened and he heard them too. His eyes went wide like mine, and he reached out to tell a security guy standing nearby. The moment he made contact with the security guard, the man fell on the floor and began to weep from the sound of the angels singing. The awareness of the spirit world was being transferred through impartation or touch similar to the account of how Elisha opened his servant's spiritual eyes.*

God's voice is the sound of many waters. He is speaking in many different ways, through our various receptors and on multiple frequencies. His voice is as many waters because He wants us to connect with Him in whatever "stream" we are dialed into. I realize that hearing God speak audibly to us isn't always necessarily up to us. Yes, we are responsible for recognizing when He does speak audibly, but we cannot force Him to speak to us that way. He is His own Person, and He gets to choose how to communicate with us. I say this to encourage you to not feel any disappointment or confusion if you are not hearing God speak audibly to you. Remember, it does not make you a "higher-level" spiritual person to hear God's voice audibly. God is speaking in multiple ways, and all of them are spiritual and deeply personal. Multiple times in scripture Jesus called out to those who would pay attention, *"Let he who has ears to hear, hear what the Spirit is saying...."*[69] God is looking for the hungry listener. He is looking for those who will hear His voice speak through the natural, internal, and heavenly realm and then to respond.

---

69  Matthew 11:5, 13:9, Revelations 2:7

# CHAPTER 9

## EXTERNAL FEELING/SENSING

*Spiritual Insights through our external senses*
*in the Natural Realm*

O UR SENSES ARE NOT GIVEN to us just to relate to the physical world, they are also powerful receptors that we
possess to give us spiritual intel. Remember, Christ died for *all*
of you–body, soul, and spirit–not just the seemingly "spiritual"
parts. Your entire being was included in the redemption package of Christ. And *each part* of you is hardwired to commune
with Him, including your senses. We have covered both seeing
and hearing extensively in the prior chapters, but over the next
three chapters, we'll focus our attention on the remaining physical senses—taste, smell, and touch, which are grouped together
as our feeling or sensing receptors.

The author of Hebrews tells us that "...*solid food is for the mature, who because of practice have their senses trained to discern good and
evil.*"[70] God's heart and will is for us to be mature sons and daugh-

---

70    Hebrews 5:14

ters. One of the ways we grow in maturity is to regularly exercise our ability to receive *through our bodily senses* and to distinguish between what is good and what is evil.

The Greek word for *practice* in this passage is *gymnazo* which means to *exercise vigorously*.[71] Think of it like this. When you practice your innate ability to know God's voice, it's like you are taking all of your receptors to the "spirit gym." When you regularly and consistently exercise your different receptor "muscles," you are strengthening your capacity to recognize God's voice in the myriad of ways He is communicating. What happens when you only exercise one of your receptors? The image that comes to mind is like those power-lifting muscle men, who are stacked in their upper body like Arnold Schwarzenegger but have tiny birdie legs. It's out of balance, awkward, and a little bit hilarious looking. We become strengthened and mature through the steady practicing of *all* the ways we are hard-wired to discern His voice.

God gave us senses not only to relate to the physical world around us but also to make us sensitive to spiritual information, and it is our duty to allow our senses to be sensitized to the voice of God. Let's explore some of the ways God speaks to us through our external senses in the natural realm around us.

## *Communion* (Taste)

Have you ever heard the phrase, *"You eat with your eyes first?"* The implication is that before a single flavor touches your lips, you are already engaging with the experience of tasting through your eyes. Perhaps this is why often in a cooking con-

---

71  https://www.blueletterbible.org/lang/lexicon/lexicon.cfm?        Strongs
    =G1128&t=NASB

test, the contestants are judged on food presentation not just taste.

Scripture declares that a form of tasting is seeing: *"Taste and see that the Lord is good."*[72] I used to only read this particular verse as metaphorical. However, as I've grown in understanding the various ways God speaks to me, I have found that all of our senses—including taste—are a powerful avenue through which God is revealing Himself to us. One of the most practical ways that we as believers participate in physically tasting and drinking in response to His voice is communion.

> *And he(Jesus) took bread, gave thanks and broke it, and gave it to them, saying, 'This is my body given for you; do this in remembrance of me.' In the same way, after the supper he took the cup, saying, 'This cup is the new covenant in my blood, which is poured out for you.'*
>
> *Luke 22:19-20*

It was His voice that spoke those words thousands of years ago, and He is still speaking today. Every time we partake of communion, the physical eating and drinking of bread and wine or juice, we are fulfilling Jesus' commands. This is one of the ways we practically interact with God's voice through taste because we are responding to something He already said. It's not enough to just hear what He says. We must also respond to what He says.

Communion is a beautiful expression of responding to His voice through our sense receptor. When we regularly connect with God through communion, His voice in our life comes alive

---

72    Psalms 34:8

fresh and new. In every bite of the communion bread, He reminds us that we are forgiven, that He has already taken our punishment upon Himself. Through every sip of the communion wine or juice, His voice resonates through our entire being that we now have resurrection in our veins through the blood of Jesus, and we are now fully alive in Him. What an amazing experience! What a wonderful way to continually hear the voice of God, reiterating His promises to us through our sense of taste! The next time you participate in communion, I encourage you to practice an intentional awareness that His voice is speaking afresh and anew to you through this sensory practice.

## *Fragrance*

Fragrance can also function as a powerful source of divine information. Did you know that while your taste buds interpret five main flavors of salty, sweet, sour, bitter, and savory, your 400 olfactory senses (relating to sense of smell) can pick up over one trillion different fragrances? A study conducted at the Rockefeller University in New York has shown that people recall 35% of what they smell, compared to only 5% of what they see, 2% of what they hear, and 1% of that they touch.[73]

One of the most consistent examples of regularly communing with God in this external sensory way is incense. Frequently throughout both the Old and New Testaments, we see the Israelites were told to regularly give an offering of incense or a fragrant offering to the Lord. The altar of incense was placed in Moses' Tabernacle and was positioned

---

73   https://www.alyssaashley.com/blogs/lifestyle/perfume-and- personality

before the veil that separated the Holy Place from the Holy of Holies.[74] Aaron was to burn incense every morning and every evening to the Lord for generations to come.[75] The twenty-four elders before the throne of God are each holding a harp and a bowl of incense. Why would God care about this sweet fragrance of incense? Because incense was a manifestation of the prayers of God's people. David said in Psalms, *"May my prayer be set before you like incense,"*[76] and the book of Revelation connects the prayers of the saints directly with incense.[77]

We also have the example of Mary pouring out the expensive bottle of perfume at the feet of Jesus a week before His crucifixion: *"She poured it on Jesus' feet and wiped them with her hair. The house was filled with the sweet smell of the perfume."*[78] Some of the disciples were angry that she wasted this expensive perfume on something as 'frivolous' as pouring it on Jesus' feet. The more appropriate gesture, according to Judas the money-keeper, was to sell the perfume to give to the poor. However, Jesus defended her actions because He knew what she was doing was in preparation for His upcoming burial. He understood her sacrifice, and it was all connected to the costly fragrance.

In the same way that there are trillions of fragrances, God describes every person and every life as having their own unique fragrance. *"For we are a fragrance of Christ to God."*[79] Though we

---

74     Exodus 30

75     Exodus 30: 7-8

76     Psalms 141:2

77     Revelations 5:8

78     John 12:3

79     II Corinthians 2:15

will explore this passage more in-depth in the next chapter, it still remains that we all carry fragrances–both natural and spiritual–that communicate to the world around us and to God.

Isaac smelled the garments of his son Jacob–thinking he was Esau–and declared, *"See, the smell of my son is as the smell of a field that the Lord has blessed!"*[80] Here, we see the fragrance of the field spoke to Isaac as the favor and blessing from the Lord. I love the smell of new books as I walk into a new bookstore. This fragrance isn't just a pleasant fragrance to me as I believe it's connected to my love of learning and who God has created me to be. It means and communicates something more meaningful.

Even the lack of smell that *should* be there can speak of spiritual realities. We find this in Daniel's recounting of the story of Shadrach, Meshach and Abednego, who were thrown unjustly into the fiery furnace. Miraculously, their bodies were not burned and the Bible says, *"...the hair of their heads was not singed, their cloaks were not harmed, and no smell of fire had come upon them."*[81] Not only were their bodies untouched by fire, they did not even smell like burnt BBQ which revealed that their God was the true God–greater than any other god of the Babylonians. The scent that *should* have been on them was not, which was a sign of God's deliverance.

Fragrances have meaning, and every created thing has a fragrance. Just as fragrance can represent our lives, prayers, and substance to God, it can also disclose God's heart and thoughts to us. Everything in creation can be a catalyst for His voice in our lives and even fragrances can speak to those willing to pay attention.

---

80   Genesis 27:27

81   Daniel 3:27

# CHAPTER 10

## INTERNAL FEELING

*God Speaking through our Internal Feelings*

M ANY HAVE EITHER downplayed or put little weight on their feelings and senses, perhaps thinking that relying on feelings is either bad or not to be trusted. However, it's important to remember that feelings and emotions are good gifts given to us by a good Father with the purpose of revealing information. What you interpret from the information you receive through your feelings and senses give you direction.

For example, many interpret feelings of anger as always being a bad emotion, but even God Himself gets angry so we know the emotion itself isn't evil. Anger, in essence, is just information telling you that some value, belief, or boundary you hold has been violated. Think of it like the warning lights on your car's dashboard. When the oil light goes on, it is indicating that you are low on oil and need to get it checked. The indicator is objective information to help you discern what to do. Likewise, the anger you feel is an objective indicator(though at the time it may not feel very objective), but how you process your anger is your responsibility.

There is not a simple answer to the questions of whether our feelings are good or bad. No person should trust their feelings above what they know is right or wrong, and they should never be chosen over what the word of God says or what the character and nature of God reveals. However, neither should we deny or suppress our feelings. Our feelings are one of our God-given receptors that can reveal His voice and heart. Let's discover some practical ways of how God communicates to us through this wonderful internal dimension of feeling and sensing.

## Compassion

Have you ever suddenly had an overwhelming sense of compassion come over you for someone? I'm not talking about those who have a gift of mercy or maybe are pastoral by nature or even those who walk around with their heart on their sleeves for all to see. I'm also not referring to a natural innate compassion that's part of your unique personality or nature. I'm talking more about a sudden, unexplainable compassion that compels you to act? Jesus did. In fact, scripture records several instances where Jesus was "moved with compassion."

*Moved with compassion, Jesus touched their eyes; and immediately they regained their sight and followed Him.*
*Matthew 20:34*

*Moved with compassion, Jesus stretched out His hand and touched him, and said to him, 'I am willing; be cleansed.'*
*Mark 1:41*

> *When Jesus went ashore, He saw a large crowd, and **He***
> ***felt compassion** for them because they were like sheep with-*
> *out a shepherd; and He began to teach them many things.*
>
> *Mark 6:34*

Notice how in each of these circumstances, it was Jesus' compassion that revealed the heart and voice of the Father and compelled Him to act accordingly. His compassion compelled Him to heal, teach, and lead. Sometimes we are so caught up in thinking God only speaks in words or visions that we forget He also communicates through our senses; and, unfortunately, we don't respond. God's voice is also revealed through His heart. We may not always *hear* what He is saying, but if we can *feel* what He is feeling, we can rightly discern what He is communicating with us.

Years ago, I was at our local grocery store, quickly grabbing a few needed items while my older children waited in the car. As I was checking out, I noticed a young couple at the customer service desk speaking with a grocery clerk. When I saw them, I suddenly felt this overwhelming sense of compassion towards them though there was no external indicator of why I would feel that way. They didn't look homeless or poor or anything– just an average young couple having a conversation with a store employee. Because I was in a hurry, I quickly finished checking out and started walking out to my car. As I was crossing the store parking lot, I looked up and noticed the same young couple walking towards the bank at the other end of the parking lot. Again, I felt that same tug of unexplainable compassion towards them. Because I had a carful of kids and groceries that needed to get home, I dismissed that internal sensing, got in my car, and began driving away.

About a mile down the road, I knew I had to go back and find that couple as the deep compassion for them would not lift. I was compelled to act. I told my kids I needed to do one other thing, turned the car around, and parked in front of the bank that this young couple had gone into. As I walked into the door, I noticed they were at the teller's station speaking with the banker. Again, they did not look necessarily distraught, but I felt something was going on with them.

They finally finished their banking business and walked out the door to leave. I mustered up my courage and went after them. As I approached them, I said, *"Excuse me. I noticed you in the grocery store, and I can't help but feel for you guys. Can I ask if you are ok? Is anything wrong or can I help you?"* As I said those words, they looked at each other with a deep sadness in their eyes and then proceeded to tell me they had just had a miscarriage that very morning. This was their first baby, and the woman had been about four months pregnant when she miscarried.

Now that I was closer to them, I could see the look of grief and sorrow on their faces and suddenly the unexplainable compassion I felt for them made sense. At that moment, I was able to pray for them, their unborn baby, as well as any future children they would have. It was an opportunity to reveal the heart of the Father for this couple even though I had no idea what their current relationship with God was. Regardless of where they were in their walk with Him, God wanted them to know that in this very dark moment of their life, He loved and cared for them.

Jesus was moved with compassion. It was His internal feelings that were revealing God's heart for a particular person, crowd or situation, and He is still speaking this way today. Often when we have these sudden, strong feelings of compassion for someone or something, there is an action point that is attached to it. Jesus didn't just experience compassion and do nothing about it. His compassion led Him to reach out to heal, deliver, and teach. The Father's compassion for the people compelled Jesus to do something, and it is the same with us. I could not let this young couple go without revealing the Father's heart for them in their situation. When God speaks to us through this unexplainable compassion, it compels us to act.

## *Internal Fragrance and Taste*

Just as with our external feeling/sensing receptors where we can gain spiritual insights through our physical sense of taste, smell, or touch, God also speaks to us through our internal senses of taste, fragrance, or touch. Let me demonstrate.

Right now, wherever you are, I want you to imagine smelling a rose or perhaps jasmine. Can you smell it? If you've smelled a rose or jasmine before, you should be able to invoke a sense of the sweet fragrance even though you're not physically smelling it. Why is that? As we learned in the last chapter, fragrance is connected to memory, and if you've smelled a rose in the past, it makes an imprint in your memory so you can remember the general fragrance of a rose.

Our ability to internally discern a fragrance or taste is a valuable addition to our understanding of perceiving spiritual information. In the same way we must *look* to see or actively *listen* to recognize God's voice; *intentionality* is key here. For many, they have not recognized God speaking to them this way because they've never intentionally tried.

A few years ago, I was at a church speaking and training on the different ways we can recognize God speaking. When we got to the part of the training on the internal sense of fragrance and taste, there were a couple men who were skeptical. They had been open and actively participating in the portion on seeing and hearing, but when we started practicing in this particular receptor, they seemed unconvinced. Does God *really* speak through our internal sense of fragrance or taste? Well, they decided to just give it a shot, and the one man said to the other, *"I don't know, but I get the impression of the taste of honey."* The other man looked at him incredulously and said, *"I'm a beekeeper!"* Needless to say, in that moment, both of these skeptics became believers that God can and does speak to us in this way.

At another training event, there was a young woman who internally smelled *salsa* over another woman and was impressed to share that the Lord was bringing this older woman into a new season, and things were going to be fresh and new. What was fun about this impression is that the receiver of the word was not only a Latina, she was also a ballroom dancing instructor, and salsa dancing was her absolute favorite type of dance. This internal fragrance impression was personally very encouraging to her and made her feel loved, seen, and known by God in a powerful way.

## Intuition

Have you ever had an intuition or gut impression about someone you've just met? Perhaps you've had a hunch or had a "sixth-sense" about something where you sense information without any external logical explanation. Most people would say they've experienced a gut feeling about a person, place, or thing at some point in their life. A gut feeling or intuition by definition *is an immediate basic feeling or reaction without a logical rationale.*

As a business owner, there have been several situations where we have had an applicant who looked like the right fit on the outside, but I had a gut impression that he or she could be trouble. Unfortunately, we had to learn the hard way that my instinct was correct when we discovered that after hiring those particular employees I had originally had a check about, they ultimately ended up being lazy, entitled or dishonest, and we had to eventually let them go. Since then, we have learned to pay attention to those internal gut impressions and recognize them as the voice of God leading us through our internal feeling receptors, especially when searching for good, solid workers for the business.

Psalms 23 tells us that He is the Good Shepherd who leads and guides us on good paths with His rod and staff. What are these tools used for in shepherding? Leading, prodding when we get off track, and protection from harm. Think of our gut impressions as a proverbial "rod" that is evidence of His presence and voice in our lives to give direction and provide for our protection and safety. Remember, God is always for you. He cares deeply about your livelihood, your business, your families, and everything that pertains to the abundant life He has promised.[82] Because we are learning to access His voice in all dimensions, we can understand that He does speak through intuitions and gut impressions.

---

82   John 10:10

# CHAPTER 11

## MYSTICAL FEELING/SENSING

*Discerning and feeling the Spirit Realm*
*with your physical senses*

T HIS CHAPTER WAS PROBABLY the most difficult for me to write because I personally have had very little experience in this particular way of encountering God's voice although I know several people who have. Regardless of my inexperience in this area, the truth is we see multiple encounters between mankind and the spirit realm in scriptures, and this makes me hungry to know Him in ways that I know is possible to me. How do I know it's possible? Because the Book of Revelation says that the testimony of Jesus is the spirit of prophecy,[83] and what He did for someone else, He can do for me. I cannot be complacent with my current level of knowing His voice when I know there is more available to me.

We are hardwired to physically feel and experience God's voice and heart through the natural, created realm. But we are

---

83    Revelations 19:10

also designed to experience the spirit realm through our physical senses. We can taste, smell and touch things from a Heavenly realm. Let's look at a few biblical examples that demonstrate this unique way of accessing the voice of God.

1) An entire generation of Israelites literally *ate* bread from heaven in the wilderness. *"Then the Lord said to Moses, 'I will rain down bread from heaven for you...' The people of Israel called the bread manna. It was white like coriander seed and tasted like wafers made with honey." (Exodus 16:4, 31)*

2) The prophet Elijah, weary from running for his life, was woken up by an angel *touching* him. *"Then he lay down under the bush and fell asleep. All at once an angel touched him and said, 'Get up and eat.'" (I Kings 19:5)*

3) Ezekiel was commanded to *eat* a scroll which was described as honey in his mouth. *"And He(God) said to me, 'Son of man, eat what is before you, eat this scroll; then go and speak to the people of Israel.' So I opened my mouth, and he gave me the scroll to eat. Then he said to me, 'Son of man, eat this scroll I am giving you and fill your stomach with it.' So I ate it, and it tasted as sweet as honey in my mouth." (Ezekiel 3:1-3)*

4) When Peter and the apostles were thrown into prison, an angel came and physically opened the doors for them. *"But during the night an angel of the Lord opened the doors of the jail and brought them out." (Acts 5:19)*

We could go on and on as the Bible is full of mystical encounters with mankind, but the point I want to make is this– God has been and *still is* regularly connecting with us in both physical and mystical ways. Let's look at some practical ways we can recognize God speaking through our own mystical feeling/sensing receptors.

## *Mystical Touch*

Frequently throughout scripture, we see the unseen realm physically collide with the seen realm. Look at just a few biblical examples below of how different people physically felt a touch from an angel.

- **Daniel**: *"Now while he was talking with me, I sank into a deep sleep with my face to the ground; but **he touched me and made me stand upright.**"*[84]

- **Jeremiah**: *"Then the Lord stretched out His hand and **touched my mouth.**"*[85]

- **Elijah**: *"Then he lay down under the bush and fell asleep. All at once **an angel touched him** and said, 'Get up and eat.'"*[86]

- **Peter**: *"Suddenly an angel of the Lord appeared and a light shone in the cell. **He struck Peter on the side and woke him up.** 'Quick, get up!' he said, and the chains fell off Peter's wrists."*[87]

Each of these and so many more examples in scriptures reveal Heaven's intent to connect and interact with mankind even in a mystical and physical way.

---

84    Daniel 8:18

85    Jeremiah 1:9

86    I Kings 19:5

87    Acts 12:7

## *Taste*

How many scriptures have we read that speak of physically experiencing spiritual realities, and yet we have ascribed them to metaphors only? For example, *"Taste and see that the Lord is good..."*[88] What if there are actually dimensions of experiencing and sensing in the spirit realm that we are discounting as only symbolic? What if it's not either/or but both/and? What if these scriptures are both speaking symbolically in the spirit realm but also revealing the possibility of these spiritual delights being available to our physical beings now? Let's look at a few more passages that we may have interpreted as metaphoric only with the possibility of truly experiencing it mystically.

> *How sweet are your words to my taste! Yes, sweeter than honey to my mouth!*
>
> *Psalm 119:103*

> *He said to me, 'Son of man, feed your stomach and fill your body with this scroll which I am giving you. Then I ate it, and it was sweet as honey in my mouth.'*
>
> *Ezekiel 3:3*

> *I took the little book out of the angel's hand and ate it, and in my mouth it was sweet as honey; and when I had eaten it, my stomach was made bitter.*
>
> *Revelation 10:10*

---

88  Psalms 34:8

Sometimes we can forget that the people we read about in the bible were humans who lived their lives day to day like we do. Yet, here we see David, Ezekiel and John the Beloved all physically tasting spiritual realities. We may not have a grid for comphending this but that's ok. God's ways are higher and far above and beyond all we can think, ask and imagine. Let's learn to accept that what we may think as impossible is just nourishment and food from a heavenly perspective. We *can* taste and see the goodness of God and thus experience His voice, heart, will or thoughts in this mystically tangible way.

## *Fragrance*

Have you ever been in a worship service that was particularly anointed and suddenly a sweet aroma filled the air? I remember a time at my church when we were praying for the nations. As I was walking around the various prayer stations, suddenly there was this fragrant, flowery "spring-like" fragrance in the air. It was not overpowering like a woman who had put on too much perfume, but rather it was light and refreshing. I walked around in a perimeter to discern the source of the fragrance. I even discreetly invaded the personal space of a few people to see if they were wearing that fragrance, but there was no logical source of the aroma. I then knew I was smelling a spiritual fragrance that was a result of the prayers being lifted up in that place.

Did you know that the phrase *a pleasing aroma* or *fragrance* appears over forty times throughout scripture? Hosea tells us that the fragrance of the coming Messiah is *like the cedars of Lebanon.*[89] Paul thanked the Philippians for their generous gift given

89  Hosea 14:6

to him and described them as a *"fragrant offering, an acceptable sacrifice to God." [90]* Every person also carries a distinct fragrance that is spiritual.

> *But thanks be to God, who always leads us as captives in Christ's triumphal procession and uses us to spread the aroma of the knowledge of him everywhere. For we are a **fragrance of Christ** to God among those that are being saved and among those who are perishing; to the one an **aroma from death** to death, to the other an **aroma from life** to life."*
>
> II Corinthians 2:14-16

Fragrances are indicators of something tangible that's present whether seen or unseen. Listen to this testimony of someone who has learned to recognize certain fragrances as the presence of angels that God has sent to help them.

> *I've been smelling what I'm quite sure is angelic presence on a very regular basis. I've been aware of this for about a year or more. A few months ago, our furnace stopped working. Because it was a Saturday, we decided to use electric heaters and wait to call the service man until Monday as that was going to be less expensive. Several hours into this day, I walked past the room with the furnace in it. I could smell a very strong fragrance, one I've become familiar with as angelic. I said out loud, 'Oh, you are there. Great!' Shortly after that encounter with the angelic fragrance, our furnace began to work and has been working great since then.*

---

90    Philippians 4:18

Why would God send an angel to fix a furnace? I believe that if it matters to you, it matters to God. Things that are important to you and your life are important to God because He is a good Father, and He cares for you. Remember, angels are sent to us as *ministering spirits*,[91] and in this instance, an angel was sent (preceded by a fragrance) to minister to their very real need for heat.

Interestingly, as we observed in the last passage, we can see that spiritual realities have a fragrance, both good and bad. I have a friend who was driving one day and began thinking about something that was frustrating to her. As she was thinking about this situation, she began complaining to the Lord about it. Suddenly, her car began to smell like rotten-eggs. The fragrance was so intense she looked around to see if she might have driven past a sewage plant or some other source of the foul smell. When she saw there was nothing that could indicate the sudden smell in her vehicle, she asked the Lord about it. She heard the Lord say, *I am allowing you to physically smell what your complaining thoughts are creating.* She literally could smell her "stinking thinking!" When she realized what was happening, she quickly repented of her "stinky" thoughts, and as quickly as the foul odor came, it left and her car smelled normal once again.

Our very lives are carrying fragrances that can be discernible by the spirit wherever we go. What fragrance are you carrying? Is it one of death that is a result of our unbelief, complaining, grumbling, or even our "stinking thinking," or is it a fragrance of life that flows from righteousness, peace, and joy? We are created to be the sweet-smelling fragrance of Christ to the world around us, and who we are in Him is pleasing to the Father.

---

91  Hebrews 1:14

## *Supernatural Adrenaline Rush*

A friend of mine had an unusual experience with his sensory receptors which God used to protect him. When he was a young man, he would encounter many near-death experiences through no fault of his own. These were crazy situations like earthquakes, car accidents, and even hurricanes where he just happened to be in the right place at the right time. Or maybe, he was actually at the wrong place at the wrong time? Either way, he recounts how immediately before something dangerous and threatening would happen, he would suddenly get an adrenaline rush. His entire body would become hyper-alert, and his sense of time would slow down. Everything would go into slow motion like you would see in the movies, and this would allow him to make decisions in the moment that would protect him. It wasn't until after this phenomenon happened several times that he began to recognize it was the Lord alerting him to a coming potential threat. Once he recognized that an adrenaline rush was the Lord speaking to him, he began paying attention and being prepared for what was to come. Thankfully, it has been many decades now of him facing life-threatening situations, but you can see how the Lord spoke to my friend through this unique mystical feeling receptor, and He can do the same for us.

## *Goosebumps or 'God Bumps'*

Goosebumps or "chicken skin," is a phenomenon that happens when the muscles under the hair follicles are raised up to look like hundreds of little bumps, mostly occurring on your arms, legs and torso.[92] Have you ever had goosebumps? Perhaps you've experienced it being in the refrigerator section of your local grocery store or stepping outside on a cold winter's morning. Your skin is the largest organ and sensor on your body, and your sense of feeling through your hair follicles is called your *mechanoreception*. Through practice as commanded by the writer in Hebrews to train *to distinguish good from evil,*[93] you can discern spiritual information even through your skin.

I have been in worship services where suddenly my arm would tingle with goosebumps or I'd feel a tickle down the back of my neck like something was being poured lightly on my head. When this happens to us, our skin is confirming information that we are receiving, which is often spiritual, not just natural. Our physical bodies are responding to God speaking something to us that our spirits are bearing witness to, often before our mind catches on. We often like to call this phenomenon 'God bumps.'

Or how about this? Have you ever experienced watching a scary movie or encountering something nasty or creepy, and you would say something like, *"Ooh, that made my skin crawl!'* What made your skin crawl? What is happening there? It's actually your skin discerning an evil spirit or an evil intent. How is it helpful for us to discern evil? God cares about your safety and protection, and often He will allow us to discern things meant to harm or hurt us so we can respond with wisdom.

Remember that the senses/feelings are receptors for spiritual information, and it is up to us to ask the Lord what to do with it and respond accordingly. When I have experienced

---

92    https://www.scientificamerican.com/article/why-do-humans-get-goosebu
      /#:~:text=Goosebumps%20are%20tiny%20elevations%20of,are%20
      attached%20to%20each%20hair.

93    Hebrews 5:14

these senses in the past without any logical or natural reason to explain it, I have learned to thank God for His presence and press into more of what He is releasing or speaking.

## *Burning Heart*

How many of you have ever felt your heart burning within you, particularly when God was speaking or revealing something weighty to you? Maybe you felt it during your salvation experience when someone was sharing the good news of the gospel to you. Perhaps it happened during a call to identity and destiny when the preacher was looking for those who would go to the nations or go to the lost on behalf of the Lord. Maybe it happened when you were reading the scriptures, and God highlighted a particular passage to you that caused your heart to burn in response. All of these ways are practical examples of how God speaks to us through our internal senses receptor.

Biblically, this sense of a "burning heart" is beautifully displayed in the story of the disciples on the road to Emmaus. Let's set the context to better understand this subject.

Jesus had just died and risen but had not yet ascended to Heaven, so there was still some confusion and doubt as to whether He was truly alive or not. Two unnamed disciples were walking towards the town of Emmaus, discussing some of the reports they had heard about Jesus when the subject Himself walked up to them. They did not recognize Jesus, which in itself is interesting as they were not *looking to see* Him in their physical surroundings even when He literally and physically showed up. How many times has Jesus come and spoken to us through our physical surroundings, but because of preconceived mindsets or beliefs, we don't recognize Him or His voice?

Back to our story. Jesus recognized that they are feeling downcast about something and asked them about it. Incredulously they responded, *"Are you the only one visiting Jerusalem who does not know the things that have happened there in these days?"* [94] The disciples then gave Jesus the updated report on all that had been going on to which Jesus proceeded to explain to them from the Scriptures, concerning Himself.

When they reached their destination, Jesus acted as if He was going to continue on, but the two disillusioned disciples pleaded for Him to stay with them even though they still had no idea it was Jesus. Jesus agreed, and as He was dining with them, the Bible records that

> . . . he(Jesus) took bread, gave thanks, broke it and began to give it to them. Then their eyes were opened and they recognized him, and he disappeared from their sight. They asked each other, 'Were not our hearts burning within us while he talked with us on the road and opened the Scriptures to us?'
>
> Luke 24:27-32

What was their reaction to Jesus' presence with them? *Were not our hearts burning within us while he talked with us...?* Their hearts were internally overwhelmed with a sense of burning. The prophet Jeremiah also described a similar sensation in context of his own call and assignment:

> But if I say, 'I will not mention his word or speak anymore in his name,' his word is in my heart like a fire, a fire

---

94   Luke 24:18

*shut up in my bones. I am weary of holding it in; indeed, I cannot.*

*Jeremiah 20:9*

The ancient prophet could literally not be silent because the word of God within him was like *fire shut up in his bones,* and to hold His word back would have been too exhausting to him. It's almost as if the pressure on the inside got so intense, he would have burst if he didn't respond to God's voice.

Years ago, I encountered this God-sense of a burning heart that I will never forget. I had gone on a road trip to just get quiet and be refreshed in the Lord. There was no conference I was attending or specific purpose for the trip other than to get into a local prayer house and soak in His presence. I remember one night as I was laying on my bed in my hotel room, the Lord illuminated something in my life He wanted me to respond to. The feeling was so intense internally. It was as if God was putting His finger on an area in my life, and I could almost feel the "heat" of His presence. As the night wore on, sleep eluded me and the internal pressure continued to escalate. I felt like I was about to explode from the inside out. My heart was burning with His voice. The next day, the feeling had not lifted, and just as Jeremiah did, I set my heart on responding to His voice. The minute I obeyed, the pressure lifted. It was like my response to His voice was a pressure valve release.

In my experience, this way of experiencing God's voice is deeply personal and connected to His word as seen with both Jeremiah the prophet and the disciples on the road to Emmaus. It can also be a response to something He is calling us to do. Either way, this burning heart sensation is a powerful way that God communicates His heart, and, therefore, His voice to us.

As with all receptors, our ability to recognize God speaking to us through our mystical sense of taste, smell, and touch allows us to regularly commune with Him. Our awareness of His voice in these areas will increase our ability to know His voice, His heart, and even His protection in our lives moving forward.

# CHAPTER 12

## EXTERNAL PERCEIVING

*Perceiving Spiritually through the Natural Realm*

O NE OF THE MORE COMMON intuitive receptors but probably less recognized in the realm of accessing God's voice
is our perceiving receptor. Oftentimes, our ability to perceive or become aware of things comes through using our various senses of
sight, hearing, and smell. For example, when you walk into your
kitchen in the morning, you may perceive it is time for the trash
to go out by what your sense of smell is telling you. This type of
perceiving often works in tandem with our other senses. However,
there is another definition of perceiving that is related to the mind
or heart, and this is where we *become aware or conscious of something;
come to realize or understand.* Also, to *interpret or look on someone or
something in a particular way.*[95] These definitions are important to
clarify as we explore how our perceiving receptor receives divine information and revelation from the Lord.

In the gospel of Luke, we see how Jesus perceived the
thoughts of the Pharisees. As they were questioning in their

---

95   https://www.lexico.com/en/definition/perceive

minds about Jesus' ability to forgive sins, Jesus didn't wait for them to verbalize their doubts before He answered their questions.

> But when Jesus perceived their thoughts, He answered
> and said to them, 'Why are you reasoning in your hearts?'
>
> Luke 5:22

The NIV translation of this verse says that Jesus *knew what they were thinking.* Jesus was receiving spiritual information in this circumstance not by seeing, hearing, or sensing, but through perceiving; and we are hardwired with the same capacity. The Greek word for perceiving in this passage is *epinigosko* which is defined as *to become thoroughly acquainted with; to know accurately; to know thoroughly.*[96] Simply put, perceiving is knowing something in your "knower." Have you ever experienced where you suddenly know something without any physical proof or logical reasoning? You don't know why you know it; you just do. It's like you *know that you know that you know* before having external confirmation on what you know.

In this chapter, we will be exploring the external perceiving receptor which is the ability to *perceive* spiritual information through the natural realm around us. To clarify, whereas our seeing receptors are connected to our eyes, the hearing is related to our ears, and the sensing/feeling receptors are attached to our sense of taste, touch and smell, the perceiving receptor is linked with our heart. Let's explore some of the ways that we can recognize God speaking through our external "knower."

---

96   https://www.blueletterbible.org/lang/lexicon/lexicon.cfm?        Strongs
     =G1921&t=NASB20

## *Countenance and Appearance*

Have you ever *people-watched* before? Perhaps you are hanging out at a coffee shop, drinking your venti latte, and looking around at the other people—obviously, not in a creepy, stalking kind of way but rather out of human curiosity. It can be very entertaining to say the least. One of my favorite places to casually observe other people is at the airport. Some of the characters and personalities you run into is a testament that God, indeed, loves variety and individuality. I think it also reveals He has a sense of humor.

One of the ways that we can perceive spiritual information in the natural realm around us is in observing people's countenance. Did you know that over half of all human communication is achieved through body language while a very small percentage of what is being communicated is the actual words spoken? Therefore, though someone may be *saying* one thing, we can often *perceive* another thing—what is actually being communicated— through their body language. *Your countenance will always reveal the reality you're most aware of.*[97] The internal reality you give most attention to—both good and bad—will be reflected in your countenance. Consider the following biblical passages that reveal our ability to perceive a person's countenance and how it's related to what is going on spiritually inside of them:

> *A glad heart makes a cheerful face, but by sorrow of heart the spirit is crushed.*
>
> Proverbs 15:13

---

97    Bill Johnson quote

*Who is like the wise man and who knows the interpreta-*
*tion of a matter? A man's wisdom illumines him and causes*
*his stern face to beam.*

*Ecclesiastes 8:1*

*So the king said to me, 'Why is your face sad though you*
*are not sick? This is nothing but sadness of heart.'*

*Nehemiah 2:2*

All of the above passages suggest that what you perceive externally can reveal what's going on in a person's heart or spirit.
You may be asking how does perceiving people's countenances
help access God's voice? That's a great question. Let's find the
answer by revisiting the story of Samuel and Eli.

Previously, when we looked at Samuel's experience with
the voice of God we were viewing through the lens of Samuel's response. Now, let's shift and look at the response of
the priest Eli to the same situation. For context, God is audibly calling Samuel's name. Because he was young, Samuel had not yet learned to recognize God's voice. Therefore,
each time he heard his name being called, he would run to
his caretaker, Eli and say, *"Here I am!"* After the first two in-
cidents, Eli sent Samuel back to bed, saying that he had not
called him. It wasn't until the third time that Eli perceived—
became aware of and recognized—through the external
realm around him (Samuel running to him three times) that
God was speaking, and he was then able to teach the young
boy how to respond appropriately to the Lord. Eli did not
hear, see, or feel God's voice in this exchange; He *perceived*
that what was happening with Samuel was a God encounter
through the natural realm.

In the story of the demonized man from Gerasene, we find a tormented soul who was literally being ruled by a legion of demons and had been for many years. After Jesus casts out the demons and heals the man, an interesting exchange happens between the townspeople and Jesus after they see him. Notice how their external perceptions of the formerly demonized man's *countenance* caused an awareness and reaction from them.

> *They came to Jesus and observed (perceived) the man who had been demon-possessed sitting down, clothed and in his right mind, the very man who had had the 'legion'; and they became frightened.*
>
> *Mark 5:15-17*

When Jesus healed and delivered the insane demoniac, the people saw the man, peaceful and in his right mind, and perceived something had shifted in his personhood, and it freaked them out. You know there is something wrong with your culture when you're more disturbed by someone's peace than their torment. We can perceive what God is doing and saying through the countenances of the people around us and learn to partner with His heart and voice for their breakthrough and connection with God.

## Circumstances

Another way God speaks and uses to get our attention is through our circumstances. Remember the ancient prophet Jonah? God initially spoke to him to go to the great city of Nineveh and preach a message of repentance to it, but Jonah rebelled and ran away from this assignment. Because Jonah ignored God's voice, scripture then records that God spoke through circumstances to get Jonah's attention.

Look at the unfolding events God used to speak to Jonah: a great wind in the sea and a violent storm; the sailors tossing him overboard; a huge fish that swallows him three days and three nights in the belly of the fish until the fish spits Jonah up onto dry land. Jonah finally caught on and recognized God speaking to him through all of these circumstances and then proceeded to fulfill his original assignment.[98] God's voice resonated through every circumstance Jonah encountered leading to his repentance and response.

We can also understand through the prophet Isaiah that it is actually *our responsibility* to perceive what God is speaking through the natural realm around us.

> See, I am doing a new thing! Now it springs up; do you not **perceive** it? I am making a way in the wilderness and streams in the wasteland.
>
> Isaiah 43:19

In this passage, we are told to perceive or know that God is doing something new by observing things springing up or sprouting forth in our lives. The implication is that the new thing God is doing is already evidenced in the *springing up*. Just as an oak tree can be seen in the beginning stages of sprouting, so can we perceive what God is doing by looking for *sprouts* or in this context, seemingly small circumstances that lead to God-size realities. What new things or circumstances are *sprouting* up in your own life? Circumstances can be the guideposts to the new thing God is bringing.

---

98   Jonah 1-2

Many years ago, I was feeling discontent with my current situation. For over a decade, I had been a worship pastor, pioneered a regional ministry school, revived and oversaw the Christian school my children attended, and even pastored our local church for a short season. Needless to say, there was a lot going on. Plus, when you throw in working with difficult personalities and human dynamics, it was not a season I'd want to do over. However, in the midst of all of the victories and challenges, I learned that there is always more than enough grace for what God calls you to do.

Towards the end of that season, I began to "pass the baton" of the different ministries I was overseeing to those I could see that God was calling to take it to the next level of advancement in the Kingdom. It was a beautiful thing to see others step into their purpose as I stepped out of those arenas. The things that had kept my attention, energy, and purpose for years now belonged to others, and my calendar was opening up.

As that was taking place, I also noticed that my peers and friends were either moving away geographically or our relationships were shifting, not in a bad way but just a different level of connection. It felt like I was slowly being "unplugged" from everything around me. Unplugged from my responsibilities, my relationships, and even my purpose in the geographical area we were living.

It was these circumstances and more that God used to catch my attention to perceive that winds of transition were coming. Things were about to change. My season was about to shift just as Isaiah prophesied, and I was in a process of forgetting the former things so I could take hold of the new thing He was bringing. As a result of perceiving what God was doing in that season through the circumstances around me, I was able to prepare accordingly and hit the ground running when He moved me and my family to a new life, new ministry, and new geographical location.

*"I am doing a new thing...Do you not perceive it?"* Some of us need to perceive what God is speaking through the current circumstances in our lives. Perhaps you need to get whole and healed, or maybe it's time to rest and recharge. Maybe it's time to start that business or ministry you've been talking about but have been afraid of taking the risk. I can completely relate to that.

Years ago, a friend of mine worked for a well-respected service business. Though he was blessed with a good boss and stable income, my friend slowly started to feel a desire to begin his own service business. When his circumstances changed (i.e., he was laid off from his job because there was little work), he didn't get bitter or become a victim of his circumstances. He perceived this was God helping him take the risk to do something he had already been talking about wanting to do for over a year. He has now been running his own service business for years, a venture that has been a blessing to his family and others for over a decade.

Ecclesiastes tells us there is a time and season for every purpose under the sun, but it's up to us to perceive what season God says we are in now. And when we do, it can bring much joy, peace, and faith into our lives and others. Look at your circumstances now and perceive what God is saying through them. Ask yourself, *What is happening in my life right now? Are there any circumstances that God is trying to get my attention through or speak to me in?* He is good and has good plans for you. Are you willing to perceive what He is saying in the natural realm around you?

# CHAPTER 13

## INTERNAL PERCEIVING

*Perceiving what God is speaking in the Internal Realm*

A s WE DISCOVERED in the external perceiving realm, Jesus perceived the Pharisees' thoughts and evil intents and then responded to them as if they had verbalized those thoughts out loud. Jesus was perceiving internally (the Pharisees thoughts) what was going on spiritually by the Spirit of God within Him.

> For who **knows** a person's thoughts except their own spirit within them? In the same way **no one knows** the thoughts of God **except the Spirit of God**. What we have received is not the spirit of the world, but the Spirit who is from God, **so that we may understand** what God has freely given us.
>
> I Corinthians 2:11-12

No one can know or perceive the thoughts of God except by the Spirit of God. One of the ways we can perceive what God is saying is to access what He is thinking. We can actually *know* God's thoughts! Why is that important? It's important because His thoughts are so much higher than ours, even higher than the heavens are from the earth,[99] and the only way to access His higher-level thinking is through His Spirit. God's got the best thoughts about you on the planet, and we can know what His thoughts are through His Spirit that dwells in us. Trust me, you *want* to know what God is thinking about you. They're better than you could imagine, and you are hardwired to internally perceive the thoughts of God. The following are a few ways that we can discern God's voice through our internal knowing receptors.

## *Internal Discernment*

Sometimes our ability to internally perceive spiritual information can look like knowing something is going on inside someone that is opposite of what they are portraying externally. Proverbs says it like this, *"Laughter can conceal a heavy heart, but when laughter ends, the grief remains."*[100]

We've all walked up to a friend or family member and immediately discerned something was "off" with them, regardless of the game face they are displaying. This is an example of being hardwired to internally perceive what's going on in the world around us. I am not talking about "reading" people; however, particularly in this area, it can be a fine line. Additionally, just because you are discerning something is going on with a person does not mean it's your responsibility to address it. Again, our

---

99   Isaiah 55:8-9

100  Proverbs 14:13

job is to ask the Lord what, if anything, we should do with this information and respond accordingly.

When God reveals this spiritual information to you, it can be for many reasons. Maybe He wants you to encourage or strengthen them? Or perhaps it's not to say anything but just pray for them? Every person on the planet wants to feel known and loved by God so when God chooses to speak to you through the care of a friend or loved one, it can be a powerful expression of His voice.

As a mother, I have a particular grace for knowing what is going on internally with my children. Responding to these impressions and asking them questions has allowed me to have access to their hearts, strengthen our connection, and bring life and truth to them. They might never have said anything to me if I had not first discerned, questioned, and responded to their needs.

## *Significant or Defining Moments*

In 2018, I was invited to speak at the main Sunday service on Mother's Day at my home church, The Mission. I was excited and nervous as it was the first time I had preached from that pulpit, and I wanted to make a lasting impact. As I was pondering a message that would be relevant to this special day, an idea came to me about what the assignment of a kingdom mother looks like and how her role contributes to the family of God. Although there has been such a tremendous number of teachings and books on fathering and even God as Father, there has been a surprising lack of teaching on what a mother carries. So, I knew some clarification and redefining the mothering assignment would be helpful to the women and men attending that day.

As I was preparing the message, I had an internal 'knowing' that what I was working on was bigger than the moment. It's not that it would be insignificant for the hearers that Mother's Day, but the perception was that this message would go beyond just that Sunday. Since I *knew* and recognized from God that something was special about this message, I paid closer attention.

A few months later, I was part of a Q & A panel at a large conference that consisted of all men and myself. Being the only woman on the panel, a particular question was directed to me; and I knew at that moment, I was supposed to give a bullet-point version of the Mother's Day message I had shared just weeks earlier. After I quickly shared my encouraging answer, the conference room erupted in cheering and applause. One of the senior leaders of the conference spoke to me and declared that I would *write the book that redefined mothering in the kingdom of God.* One year later at the exact same conference, I released my first book on kingdom mothering called *Own Your Assignment*. Since that time, I have heard incredible feedback and testimonies of women breaking free from false mindsets and owning their permission to be who God says they are.

I don't share this testimony to commend myself but to give you insight into my process. I had this little message about mothering that I was going to share at my home church. Very much like the fish and loaves brought to Jesus,[101] I didn't have much, but I had something. I brought what I had, and God multiplied it. It wasn't that the message I preached that day was extra anointed or anything but that I had recognized in my internal "knower" that something about this message was bigger

---

101  Matthew 14:13-21

than what I had originally thought, and God was speaking it to me so I could be prepared.

Recognizing the ways God speaks to us is vital to our success in life. Remember that mankind was not created to be sustained on food alone but by *"every word that proceeds from the mouth of God."*[102] In life, we all have decisions to make. Learning to pay attention to these little "knowings" and recognizing that God can and does speak through them will allow us not to miss potential God-opportunities.

## *Warnings*

Have you ever had an instinct–whether good or bad–about something? Maybe you've suddenly had an internal warning that seemed to come out of nowhere. This type of perceiving is similar to the gut-feeling I spoke about in the chapter about internal senses except that this perception is more of a heart conviction than a gut feeling. I've noticed that God often speaks to our internal perceptions to communicate warnings or to help make us aware of a potential difficulty coming in the near future. In fact, this is one of the ways that God communicated an impending danger to the apostle Paul in the book of Acts.

As the story unfolds, Paul as a prisoner is being sent to Rome via sea. The journey was already slower than it should have been due to changing ships multiple times and poor weather. At one point as they anchored in a place called Fair Havens, the implication is that the captain of the ship and Roman centurions were in discussion about whether to keep going on to Rome or to stay in port through the winter. It was at this junction that Paul interjects:

102  Matthew 4:4

*Paul began to admonish them, and said to them, 'Men, **I** **perceive that the voyage will certainly be with damage** **and great loss**, not only of the cargo and the ship, but also of our lives.*

*Acts 27:9-10*

Paul *perceived* that if they continued on the journey, it would be treacherous for all involved. Paul didn't see, hear, or feel this divine information; he knew it in his *knower*. Unfortunately, both the captain of the ship and the centurion disregarded Paul's perceptions and proceeded with their travel where they indeed ended up losing the ship, cargo, everything–barely escaping with their lives.

When I was in my college years, I was dating a young man who went to a university about thirty minutes from my house. One evening, I wanted to go visit him at the college campus, but I had a problem. My car had four bald tires, and there was torrential rain outside–not a good combination. As I was processing my dilemma, I had this awareness, this knowing inside, that it would be a *really* bad idea to drive my car to see him. It was more than just common sense. It was like I had a siren going on in my knower that if I moved forward with my car, things could go very wrong.

Yet, I made a plan(If you know me, I always have a plan). I asked my mom if I could borrow her car to drive down to see him to which she emphatically replied, "No." After pleading with her and sharing the concerns about the lack of safety with my own vehicle, her solution for me was to just not go at all which I wasn't having.

So, I got in my car—four bald-tires and all—and started the thirty-minute trek. Just as I was entering onto the six-lane highway, my car began to hydroplane, doing three-hundred-and-sixty degree turns. I don't know how many times I spun on that highway, but I do remember seeing headlights out my passenger window coming toward me and crying out "*Jesus, Jesus*" as I spun out of control. Suddenly, my car stopped, facing out toward the freeway on the shoulder of the fast lane–no dents or even a scratch on my car to be seen. The only thing shaken up was me.

It wasn't until many years later that I was able to recognize that God had been trying to get my attention through my internal perceiver to make me aware of a potentially bad situation. God values our safety and cares deeply for each of us, so why wouldn't He speak about situations that could potentially bring harm to us? You are created to recognize His voice through your internal perceptions and knowing's.

# CHAPTER 14

## MYSTICAL PERCEIVING

*Perceiving spiritual information from the Spirit Realm*

PERCEIVING IN THE HEAVENLY realm looks like revealed information of knowledge from strictly spiritual sources, as opposed to earthly or internal sources. In this chapter, the fact that we are learning how we are perceiving directly from the heavenly realm as opposed from the natural/internal has more to do with the *realm* we are picking up information from, not it's spiritual impact.

Perceiving in this manner can often look like involuntary divine revelation. Meaning, you suddenly know something in your "knower" that was spiritually revealed by the Spirit. Words of knowledge are often received in this way though certainly they are not limited to our perceiving receptors only. Let me give you an example found in the book of Matthew of someone who perceived divine information from the Father Himself.

*When Jesus came to the region of Caesarea Philippi, he asked his disciples, 'Who do people say the Son of Man is?''*

> *They replied, 'Some say John the Baptist; others say Eli-*
> *jah; and still others, Jeremiah or one of the prophets.'*
>
> *'But what about you?' He asked. 'Who do you say I am?'*
>
> *Simon Peter answered, 'You are the Messiah, the Son of*
> *the living God.' Jesus replied, 'Blessed are you, Simon son*
> *of Jonah, **for this was not revealed to you by flesh and***
> ***blood, but by my Father in heaven.'***
>
> *Matthew 16:13-17*

Peter had been given a revelation that others had not yet received. He *knew* Jesus was the Messiah. This revelation did not
come from witnessing all of the miracles he had already seen or
heard. Peter knew Jesus was the Messiah because it had been
revealed to him directly by the Father Himself. Jesus even acknowledged and affirmed to Peter that the source of his revelation was divine.

The Greek definition for *revealed* in this passage is *apokalypto*
which means to *uncover, lay open what has been veiled or covered*
*up; to make known.*[103] There are things we can't know until God
unveils them to us. This is what He did for Peter. Jesus' identity
as the Messiah was previously unknown on earth until the Father laid open that truth to Peter. There are treasures of wisdom
and knowledge stored up in the person of Jesus Christ that are
waiting for their time of *unveiling.*[104]

The book of Proverbs tells us that it *is the glory of God to conceal*
*a matter, but it is the glory of kings to search it out.*[105] God hides things

---

103  https://www.blueletterbible.org/lang/lexicon/lexicon.cfm?
Strongs=G601&t=NASB20

104  Colossians 2:3

105  Proverbs 25:2

in order for them to be found. He hides treasures for those who would value it, so He can reveal it in its proper time. Think of it like an Easter egg hunt for children. The purpose of hiding the eggs is not so they can remain hidden and frustrate the children. No, it's for the challenge and delight of the child to discover something they know holds good things for them. It's the same for us and revelation. There are times when we apply ourselves to understand what He has concealed, and there are other moments where God by His grace and wisdom speaks to us, and we suddenly perceive spiritual information that we would have had no way of knowing otherwise. Let's explore some practical ways that God speaks to us through our perceiver receptor from this heavenly realm.

## *Discerning Good and Evil*

The writer of Hebrews makes an interesting connection between our senses and the spirit realm. *"But solid food is for the mature, who by constant use have trained themselves to distinguish good from evil."*[106]

The very fact that we can be *trained* to distinguish both good and evil implies that we can pick up spiritual information that is not from God. Additionally, our ability to consistently discern God's voice from other voices speaks to our spiritual maturity. The following are three primary sources of information that we are all exposed to and need to learn to distinguish between:

- God
- demonic
- human

---

106   Hebrews 5:14

Many people like to use the above verse to give them permission to look for the bad or evil in the world. Honestly, it's not very hard to discern what's wrong in a person or situation. The challenge is actually to look for the treasure–not the trash–and this is what this verse is referring to. It's essentially saying, "We are going to be exposed to darkness, but those who are *mature* will practice looking for the light of God's voice in any situation." This is what makes us mature. We are called to be treasure hunters not dumpster divers. Mature believers discern the gold of God's goodness and practice choosing to look at that.

Practically, this can look like discerning atmospheres. How many of you have ever walked into a room and before anyone has said anything, you can immediately discern what's going on spiritually? Perhaps you have walked into a church service on Sunday morning, and immediately you *know* the presence of God is in that place. Discerning atmospheres in the spirit realm allows us to know what God is up to in a particular person or place so we can partner with His will for that situation.

David did this with King Saul when he served him as a minstrel in his royal court. Saul was being tormented by an oppressive demonic spirit and was desperately seeking relief, so David was brought in to play music for him. Look what happens when David plays. *"And whenever the tormenting spirit from God troubled Saul, David would play the harp. Then Saul would feel better, and the tormenting spirit would go away."*[107] David shifted the negative, oppressive atmosphere by releasing the Spirit of God that was upon him through his worship.

Worship, in particular, seems to be a catalyst for discerning angelic activity in the atmosphere. There have been multiple

---

107   I Samuel 16:23 NLT

times I have been sitting alone at my piano just playing and worshiping the Lord when suddenly I discerned a presence behind me. It was so strong, I would look over my shoulder to see if someone had walked in unannounced, but there was no one there. Over the years, I have learned to discern that sensation as an angelic presence being near me as I worship.

As a worship leader for over twenty years, there have been countless times when I have discerned an atmosphere of hopelessness, weariness, or general discouragement in the congregation. No one had said anything to me, but I just knew what was going on. In those instances, what's important to remember is to never address the demonic spirit (e.g., despair, oppression, hopelessness) but to ask the Lord what He wants to release and go in the opposite spirit.

For example, if I'm discerning hopelessness in the room, I'm not going to sing about how people are feeling hopeless. No! I'm going to worship the Lord as our Hope and Deliverer! If people are feeling battle-weary from daily life and struggles, I'll declare and worship that the joy of the Lord is my strength! Do you see how this works? We learn to distinguish good from evil, not so we can be impressed by what the enemy is doing, but so we can bring God's kingdom and life wherever we go.

## Words of Knowledge

Words of knowledge are part of the nine manifestation gifts given by the Spirit of God found in the first book of Corinthians.

> *"To one there is given the word of wisdom through the Spirit and to another the **word of knowledge according to the same Spirit**."*
>
> *I Corinthians 12:8*

I believe words of knowledge are one of the most practical ways we perceive God's voice in the mystical realm, and God is speaking in this way more than we realize. Peter, as mentioned in the beginning of the chapter, essentially had a word of knowledge about Jesus' identity.

A couple years ago I had a word of knowledge that something wasn't right with our business taxes. The sense I had was more of a "knowing," and I couldn't shake it. We had already filed our taxes for the year, but something seemed off. So, the Lord led me on a treasure hunt to discover what was affecting my peace in this area. I sat down at my office desk and began looking through our online accounting software. Similar to searching for a needle in a haystack, the Lord kept leading me closer and closer until I found the needle. It was an accidental, fifty-thousand dollar, double-entry mistake for a job we had done which had increased our tax liability bill by over ten thousand dollars!

Needless to say, we were ecstatic to discover this money-saving mistake, and in the process, even impressed our bookkeeper at my ability to find this very random charge. How did I do it? God spoke to me. He dropped a word of knowledge into my "knower," and I searched out this matter through His Spirit, and was blessed as an outcome. Again, why would God even take the time to reveal this to me? Simply, God wants to be involved in every part of our life—our family, our marriage, our job, our business, our hobbies, our sorrows, our joys—everything. This is why you are hardwired to connect with Him. He loves you and loves doing life with you.

Years ago, my sister was unable to attend a special church service where a high-profile speaker and lover of God was ministering. She had a friend who was attending and was videoing the meeting live, so she jumped on to watch the meeting live through her friend's Facebook. Just as she accessed the video, the minister was speaking out a word of knowledge. He said he saw a *"nun who lived on Sandy Meadows Drive, possibly named Heather."* When my sister heard that, she jumped out of her seat and called her friend, who was at the meeting, hoping to reach the minister. The reason she got so excited is because her name is Heather Nunn, and she lives on Sandy Meadows Drive. This minister of the gospel had had a word of knowledge—-divine revelation of past to present information—about my sister, who wasn't even in the room.

This minister didn't know my sister, didn't know she wasn't going to be at this meeting, and didn't know any people that would have known that information. He had received this word directly from the Spirit, and though there's more to the story, my sister was radically blessed by that word. Just as he received divine information about my sister through a word of knowledge, God can and does speak to us in that way, too.

# CHAPTER 15

## KEYS FOR KNOWING HIS VOICE

T HE QUESTIONS WE GET asked the most when we train at
schools and conferences are *how do you recognize God's
voice*, and *how do I know that it's actually Him speaking and not my
own imagination or the voice of the enemy?* We love those questions
because it reveals a heart that truly wants to connect with the
Lord and not be deceived. Though there are several books and
teachings that dive deeper into this subject, I will give you four
basic principles and protocols that we use to judge if what we
are receiving is from the Lord or not.

### 1. God's voice will never contradict His character or His nature.

God will never speak to us in a way that is contrary to
Who He is. The fruit of His voice to us should always be in
alignment with the fruit of His Spirit—love, joy, peace, pa-
tience, kindness, and gentleness–the residue of His voice
should have those traits as well. For example, because He
is love, you should always feel the love of God in every exchange. Because He is kind, gentle, and lowly of heart, we

can expect that He will also speak to us this way; and when the conversation is over, you should still feel the effects of His kindness in your heart. Knowing the *way* God speaks is as important as *what* He says because He will never speak outside of His nature. If you experience anything contrary to Who He is such as fear, condemnation, accusation, or disappointment, then that is not His voice because those things are not in His nature.

> *The Lord, the Lord, the compassionate and gracious God,*
> *slow to anger, abounding in love and faithfulness, maintain-*
> *ing love to thousands, and forgiving wickedness, rebellion*
> *and sin.*
>
> *Exodus 34:6-7*

The Lord is always very clear about His nature in scripture and wants us to know He is good, compassionate, gracious, and kind. This is why knowing the Lord—who He really is, what He likes, His favorite things, the things that concern His heart, the things that please Him and bring Him joy—contribute to our right perception of Him. And, our ability to know Him and His character directly affects our ability to recognize His voice.

## 2. God's voice will never be contrary to the person of Jesus Christ.

I have a spiritual father who says *Jesus Christ is perfect theology.* What does that mean? If you want to know who God is and what He is really like, look at the person of Jesus Christ.

*The Son is the radiance of God's glory and the exact representation of his being, sustaining all things by his powerful word.*

*Hebrews 1:3*

In the same way, if you want to know what God's *voice* is like, just look at Jesus. Look at how He lived, how He interacted with those around Him, and His heart for people. Jesus is the exact representation of the Father, and by reading in the Scriptures how He operated, ministered, and connected with the world around Him, will reveal to us what God the Father's voice is like in our lives.

### 3. God's voice will never contradict Scripture.

God's voice will never contradict Scripture. He may contradict *our wrong perception or interpretation* of Scripture, but He cannot and will not speak against it. The first chapter of the gospel of John tells us that Jesus is the Word of God made flesh. To contradict Scripture would be to contradict Himself which He cannot do for that would make Him a liar, and we already know that God cannot lie.[108] Therefore, we can trust that when the Lord speaks to us, it will be within the beautiful boundaries of His Word.

That's not to say that He won't speak to things in our lives that are not mentioned in Scripture. For example, if the Lord speaks to you about buying a new car or about a job transition, technically those modern-day items are not in the Bible because obviously cars were not invented yet. But the principles of God

---

108  Numbers 23:19

giving good gifts to His children and when we *delight ourselves in the Lord, He gives us the desires of our hearts*[109] are true and found within Scripture and can apply.

If you really want to know God and His voice, I encourage you to read the Bible, not just as words on a page to mentally digest but to encounter Him as an actual Person. The Bible was never meant to be read as a historical document or as a rule-book of "do's and don'ts." When we understand and read the Bible as a relational book that shows us how to relate and connect with God and with one another, it will change how you view and interact with Him. He is good. He is love. He never changes.

## 4. God's voice should be judged in community.

Though every person on the planet is hardwired to know His voice, part of the reason many don't recognize His voice is because they don't actually know Him. They've either never met the Lord or have had negative experiences with people who have abused and tainted their perception of who God is for them.

It's also hard to recognize someone's voice if you've never been around them, and this is where community is so important. Because we are also created with a need for community, it is often within community that we get to help one another recognize and display God's voice and heart. Many pre-Christian's first encounters with the love of the Father for them was through another person. Not only do we get to *be the voice of God's heart* to others in community, we also have the opportunity to help others judge or discern whether what

---

109  Psalms 37:4

they are hearing is God's voice just as the priest Eli did with the boy Samuel.[110]

We function best in the context of a healthy community. We were never meant to be alone in this world. I like how my colleague puts it, regarding the need for community when discerning spiritual encounters: *The lone ranger becomes the weird stranger.* We've all seen people be powerful for a season, and then because of offense, bitterness, anger, or a host of other things, isolate themselves from community and get off into weird or harmful behaviors.

A healthy community helps us process what we are hearing from God to discern and grow in our ability to recognize His voice. This is especially helpful when what you may feel you are hearing causes you confusion or concern. Community keeps us grounded. It keeps us grounded in love with God and with one another and is a safeguard against being deceived by the enemy's voice.

---

110  I Samuel 3

# CHAPTER 16

## SPIRITUAL SYNESTHESIA

I N THE PRECEDING CHAPTERS, each of your spiritual receptors have been intentionally isolated to reveal the different ways that God speaks to us. The point of isolating them is to clearly understand the nuances and benefits of each receptor; however, they rarely function alone. As people recognize and expand their twelve spiritual receptors, we often find that any combination of these receptors works together to bring forth greater clarity. We call this blending of the twelve receptors "spiritual synesthesia." In scientific terms, *synesthesia* is defined as *a neurological condition in which stimulation of one sensory or cognitive pathway (for example, hearing) leads to automatic, involuntary experiences in a second sensory or cognitive pathway (such as vision). Simply put, when one sense is activated, another unrelated sense is activated at the same time.*"[111]

An example of this in human behavior is characterized by the observable phenomenon of a person who hears a certain note played on the piano and involuntarily sees a particular color. Each note on the piano produces a different color. For

111  https://www.psychologytoday.com/us/basics/synesthesia

example, when they hear the C note, they might see red, the D note—blue, the E note—green, etc. Here we see that multiple senses are blending together to produce something unique and defined.

Biblically, we can also see this concept of spiritual synesthesia. Let's look at a few scriptural examples where two or more receptors are being activated and working together.

> **Taste** *and see that the Lord is good…*
>
> *Psalms 34:8.*

> *I will* **look** *to see what he will* **say** *to me, and what answer I am to give to this complaint.*
>
> *Habakkuk 2:1*

> *In Damascus there was a disciple named Ananias. The Lord* **called** *to him in a* **vision,** *'Ananias!' 'Yes, Lord,' he answered. The Lord* **told** *him, 'Go to the house of Judas…'*
>
> *Acts 9:10*

Each of the above biblical examples show us that when the Lord spoke, it was not always in one way only. Again, this reveals the importance of having *all* of our receptors activated so that we can recognize God speaking on any frequency He is choosing to connect with us. Some people lean on their primary default receptors only without developing their ability to know God's voice in these other arenas, and it can sometimes cause frustration. For example, someone with a primary receptor of seeing will witness spiritual pictures and images but not necessarily have the understanding of what they are seeing because they need to also *hear* the interpretation. Often things we see in the spirit realm are unexplainable in natural terms; therefore, we need clarification by the Spirit to understand its meaning. We see this challenge with the prophet Ezekiel as he was attempting to explain what he was seeing in a heavenly vision:

*As I looked at the living creatures, I saw a wheel on the ground beside each creature with its four faces. This was the appearance and structure of the wheels: They sparkled like topaz, and all four looked alike. Each appeared to be made like a wheel intersecting a wheel. As they moved, they would go in any one of the four directions the creatures faced; the wheels did not change direction as the creatures went. Their rims were high and awesome, and all four rims were full of eyes all around.*[112]

Without the interpretation needed by utilizing spiritual synesthesia, often what we see, hear, taste, and know alone, can be a source of confusion for us. Here was Ezekiel doing his best to explain what he *saw* without any context for others. This reminds me of an old Indian parable about three blind men and an elephant. The story goes something like this:

*A group of blind men heard that a strange animal called an elephant had been brought to the town, but none of them were aware of its shape and form. Out of curiosity, they said: 'We must inspect and know it by touch, of which we are capable'. So, they sought it out, and when they found it, they groped about it. The first person whose hand landed on the trunk, said, 'This being is like a thick snake'. For another one whose hand reached its ear, it seemed like a kind of fan. As for another person whose hand was upon its leg, said the elephant was a pillar like a tree-trunk. The blind man who placed his hand upon its side said the elephant, "is a wall".*

---

112 Ezekiel 1:15-17

*Another who felt its tail described it as a rope. The last blind man felt its tusk, stating the elephant is that which is hard, smooth and like a spear.* [113]

Just as these blind men experienced limited perspective without greater context of the elephant, I believe this is what was happening with Ezekiel, and can often happen to us. Ezekiel had no context for understanding all that he was seeing and with the limited perspective he had, he did his best to describe the images in the spirit realm.

Because a single perception provides only partial information, this is where the importance of spiritual synesthesia comes in. To better understand, Ezekiel also needed to hear or perceive the meaning or interpretation of what he was seeing. The blending of multiple perceptions provides a more circumspect picture of what the Lord is saying, and one of the best ways to activate your other receptors is by asking the Lord questions in regards to what He is revealing. The ancient prophet Daniel knew how to seek explanation for the things he was seeing but not understanding.

*I, Daniel, was troubled in spirit, and the visions that passed through my mind disturbed me. I approached one of those standing there and asked him the meaning of all this. "So he told me and gave me the interpretation of these things...*
*Daniel 7:15-16*

Daniel was seeing a vision of things to come, and it troubled him because he did not understand the meaning of the visions

---

113 https://en.wikipedia.org/wiki/Blind_men_and_an_elephant

he was seeing. He needed help, so he asked for it. In his dream, he turned to the angel near him and asked for an interpretation, and the angel told him the meaning. Again, note the multiple receptors at work here. Daniel not only *saw* the vision but *heard* the voice of the angel. Daniel needed more than his seeing receptors to understand the profound revelation of the things to come. If these prophets needed the synergy of spiritual synesthesia to understand more fully what God was saying, how much more should we pursue the benefits provided with all of our receptors? Spiritual synesthesia is a valuable way to connect with the full voice of the Father.

I also want to interject here a quick note about "communal synesthesia." While I have been focusing on your individual ability to receive information from God, as believers, we are part of a greater Body of Christ. Each of us can receive from every spiritual receptor; however, when we combine our senses with others, we experience an exponential increase in knowing and experiencing God's voice. Scripture is clear that each one of us knows *in part*,[114] but when we bring our individual parts together, there is a synergy and clarity experienced in that communal synesthesia. Just because you can receive from every receptor doesn't mean you should isolate yourself from what others are perceiving. Yes, you can and do receive from God but that does not discount what others are receiving from Him as well. Rather, you should seek to benefit from the added information that others bring to the table that you may not see. Often, when we come together and honor what the Lord is speaking to one another, we gain a fuller picture of what He is communicating to us.

---

114   I Corinthians 13:9

# CHAPTER 17

## JESUS IS OUR MODEL

J ESUS, THE SON OF GOD, used all of His spiritual receptors. He was a seer. *"The Son can only do what He sees the Father doing."*[115] He was a hearer. *"These words you hear are not my own, they belong to the Father who sent me."*[116] As our High Priest, scripture reveals that Jesus was a feeler, who was" *touched with the feeling of our infirmities"*[117] and often was stirred to supernatural action when *moved with compassion.*[118] Jesus was also a perceiver as revealed in Luke's Gospel. *"But when Jesus perceived their thoughts, He answered and said to them . . ."*[119] Jesus is our standard, and He didn't limit Himself to communing with God through just a single receptor but modeled what is possible for all sons and daughters of God.

The book of Ephesians tells us that the goal of equipping the saints is to *"reach unity in the faith and in the knowledge of the Son of God and become mature, attaining to the whole measure of the*

---

115  John 5:19

116  John 14:24

117  Hebrews 4:15

118  Matthew 14:14

119  Luke 5:22

*fullness of Christ.*"[120] Throughout my travels and training adventures around the world, I have met many people who defined themselves by a single perception. They may say, *I am a seer* or *I am a feeler.* I understand what they mean by this. They are identifying a primary perception by which they receive spiritual information. However, I'm concerned that this type of singular identification might be dangerous territory. No believer should camp at a single perception when maturity rests in pursuing the measure of the fullness we see in the life of Jesus. I hope that this book has stimulated an exploration of a deeper understanding in knowing the ways that God speaks to you, and a clarity will emerge that will make you confident and powerful.

As you grow in your ability to see, hear, feel, and know that God is speaking to you in these various ways, be encouraged. You are *already* receiving from Him through some of these receptors as well as new opportunities to expand into new avenues of His voice. He has given you eyes to see. He *wants* you to see what He is saying. He did not create you with the ability to feel, hear, or know only to suppress His voice to you in these ways. His heart is and always has desired communion and connection with His beloved sons and daughters. He wants you to know Him on every frequency because the goal of our maturity is and always has been fullness in Christ.

There is no greater dignity for a son and daughter of God than to know the voice of their Father.[121] Cast away any doubt that you don't or can't hear Him because He has made every possible provision for you to recognize His voice. You are created for His voice. This is your God connection.

---

120  Ephesians 4:13

121  Cleddie Keith quote

To activate your God connection
please go to
**www.activateprophecy.com**

For more resources from Bethany check
out her book *Own Your Assignment*,
available on Amazon.

Made in the USA
Columbia, SC
08 February 2024

31118750R00096